THE
KEYS TO
EXCELLENCE

The story of
THE DEMING PHILOSOPHY

By Nancy R. Mann, Ph.D.

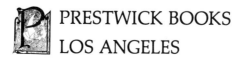

PRESTWICK BOOKS
LOS ANGELES

Library of Congress catalogue card number:
85-80370

ISBN 0-9614986-0-9

First Edition, July, 1985
Second Printing, November, 1985
Second Edition, January, 1987
Fourth Printing, October, 1987

Published in Japanese by the
Diamond Publishing Company, Tokyo

Printed in the United States of America

Gratitude is expressed to United Magazine for permission to use previously copyrighted material and to the following for permission to use photographs and other materials appearing in the photo section.

p. 73   M. L. Howley
p. 78   The Ford Motor Company
p. 79   Sumitomo Metals
p. 80   M. L. Howley
p. 81   The Nashua Corporation
p. 82   Quality Magazine
p. 83   Pontiac Motor Division, General Motors
p. 84   RV Business
p. 85   Robert Longsdorf, Jr./RV Business
p. 86   The Philadelphia Inquirer
p. 87   The Ford Motor Company
p. 88   W.E. Deming Institute, New Zealand
        U.S. Naval Air Rework Facility

Pictures not otherwise credited are from Dr. Deming's private collection.

A WORD FROM DR. DEMING

It was with pleasure and satisfaction that I learned from Dr. Nancy Mann her intention to write a book to explain to people in management about the transformation that must take place to halt the decline of Western industry and turn it upward. Management must learn what their job is and go to work on it. There is no compulsion to survive. To learn what to do and to take action can only be purely voluntary.

For a long period of time after World War II, till around 1962, the world bought whatever American industry produced. The only problem that American management faced was lack of capacity to produce enough for the market. No ability was required for management under those circumstances. There was no way to lose.

It is different now. Competition from Japan wrought challenges that Western industry was not prepared to meet. The change has been gradual and was, in fact, ignored and denied over a number of years. All the while, Western management generated explanations for decline of business that now can be described as creative. The plain fact is that management was caught off guard, unable to manage anything but an expanding market.

People in management can not learn on the job what the job of management is. Help must come from outside.

The statistician's job is to find sources of improvement and sources of trouble. This is done with the aid of the theory of probability, the characteristic that distinguishes statistical work from that of other professions. Sources of improvement, as well as sources of obstacles and inhibitors that afflict Western industry, lie in top management. Fighting fires and solving problems downstream is important, but relatively insignificant compared with the contributions that management must make. Examination of sources of improvement has brought forth the 14 points for management and an awareness of the necessity to eradicate the deadly diseases and obstacles that infest Western industry.

The transformation required for Western industry is everybody's job. A critical mass of people must understand the reasons for change and what the changes will involve. Dr. Mann, with her superb understanding of the principles to follow and with her ability as a teacher and expositor, will be able, through this book, to reach a large audience and thus build up the critical mass of people that is so necessary to assist top management to carry on the task of transformation.

ACKNOWLEDGMENTS

No book can be conceived and written by one single individual. Every author needs help of one sort or another, and I am pleased to acknowledge quite a bit of it.

First of all, there was Dr. Deming who gave me hours and hours of his time in recounting the story of his life and experiences and who provided access to others who could supplement what he told me.

Then, there was Dr. Robert Launer of the U.S. Army Research Office (A.R.O.), who saw to it that funds were made available, through UCLA from the U.S. Bureau of the Census and the U.S. Army Armament, Munitions and Chemical Command, via A.R.O., for partial support of my writing the book.

In 1986, the Office of Naval Research (ONR), through my UCLA ONR grant, helped support the work involved in preparing additions and revisions for the second edition.

Substantial parts of the contents are based on information obtained during on-site visits. Several who went beyond the call of duty in their show of hospitality during those visits were: Lloyd S. Nelson and William Conway of the Nashua Corporation, Ron Moen of General Motors, Bill Scherkenbach and Jim Bakken of the Ford Motor Company and Mr. Junji Noguchi of the Union of Japanese Scientists and Engineers (J.U.S.E.).

In addition, my sincere thanks go to Churchill Eisenhart of the U.S. Bureau of Standards. Careful research for his introduction of Dr. Deming prior to the bestowal of one of the latter's several honorary doctorates, was most helpful in supplementing material relating to Dr. Deming's early professional career.

Books are not only written, but rewritten and rewritten. Several who read early drafts and contributed toward improving the manuscript are Professor Michael Hasofer of the University of New South Wales, Australia; Ray Goldstein of Litton Industries; Lloyd S. Nelson of the Nashua Corporation; Bill Putnam of Aurum Technology, Inc., Margaret Miller of Quality Enhancement Seminars; Emanuel Berman of Berman and Berman, Ltd.; my neighbor, Fran Bishop, psychologist and former journalist; Moon Chull Han, who provides me with research assistance at UCLA, and Laura Mann, my daughter.

Avis Williams of the Biomathematics Department at UCLA patiently transcribed hours of audio tapes that were all but impossible to understand. For this she has my undying thanks.

Finally, my sincere gratitude goes to Gerard Pick, of Computer Consultants and Systems, without whose editorial expertise I would have been lost.

FOREWORD

This book is about a comprehensive philosophy for management and the man who devised it. It is about a management tool for building quality into any product, a process that leads inexorably to increased productivity and more favorable competitive position. With this style of management there are no economic tradeoffs between quality and productivity. As quality improves there will be less scrap and less rework; disgruntled, complaining customers will be replaced by happy, satisfied ones. And not only the actual users of a product, but also all of those following in the production process are considered customers to be satisfied.

From every stage of the process, information is fed to all other stages; i.e. the information flow within a production process is used with the aid of statistical tools to improve it. Designers learn from manufacturing personnel, as well as from salesmen, from those who make service calls and many, many others. Across all levels of management, there is teamwork. "Private turf" is a thing of the past.

This philosophy of excellence and continual improvement, the Deming philosophy, requires a company to buy, not from the lowest bidder, but rather from suppliers who have shown evidence that their processes produce high quality. Quality is, in fact, the over-riding management principle. Goals that pertain merely to numbers of units produced are totally eliminated. So are meaningless slogans that exhort the workers to be more productive without supplying the methods for doing so.

With this philosophy, everyone knows what his job is and is no longer hampered by poor tools or inherited defects from taking pride in his work. Everyone is trained and, when necessary, retrained. Foremen no longer have the responsibility of speeding production at any cost. Their new job is to do whatever is required to help the workers turn out an excellent product.

The book tells how the philosophy evolved. It tells how we in the U.S. were exposed to it in its embryonic form during World War II and why we failed to recognize, as Japan did, its importance to economic development. We discover how the Japanese came to see its potential rewards and why they were so successful in putting it to work. And we learn how several U.S. companies are now making this philosophy a way of life and are thereby increasing their productivity and becoming more competitive in the marketplace.

PREFACE

There are some who think we may be overwhelmed by the degree of trauma we are lately experiencing in certain areas of our lives, especially with regard to the shifting and dodging required to ensure some small degree of economic security. Folks who are mailing out "SUBSCRIBE OR RISK THE CONSEQUENCES" offers may be the principal beneficiaries of this total loss of sanity because of our fear of not staying afloat financially. But American industry may also be benefitting in an unsuspected and indirect way. The prevailing psychology seems to have precipitated the beginning of a large-scale transformation in the attitudes of industrial management concerning productivity and what must be done to increase it.

This latter phenomenon became dramatically apparent to me in early February of 1982. I had just returned from a six-day trip to Washington, D.C. to find three medium-sized mountains of mail that had been deposited on my quite sizable desk. Buried within the one shaped like Mount Olympus was a magazine with a long article about my good friend and fellow statistician, W. Edwards Deming, with whom I had spoken just five days earlier in Washington. The headline of the article read, "Japan's Rebuilder Grim on U.S. Business." It began:

"The man who revolutionized industry in Japan after

it was blown to shambles during World War II believes the days of American dominance in industrial circles are long gone.

"Dr. W. Edwards Deming, 81, offers a grim forecast for the United States in what he calls the 'new economic age.'

"'This country's industry is already destroyed,' Deming says sternly. 'The Japanese surrendered to General MacArthur in 1945. American labor surrendered to the Japanese a few months ago. We're not going to make it. The methods that made this country wealthy don't work anymore.'

"Many credit Deming with lifting war-ravaged Japan to its current dominant position in world trade. Deming agrees.

"'I did it, yes certainly,' he says. 'In 1950, I was the only man who believed that within five years, Japanese quality could capture the markets of the world.'"

Dr. Deming has wanted to tell American industry about his methods for improving quality and productivity for three decades. Until recently, very few were listening. The article noted the change in attitudes.

". . .Now American companies are flocking to the statistician as their competitive edge slips.

"'But,' he says, 'there is no quick fix available to resurrect American industry. It takes time to purge industry of outdated ideas.'

"...'Management has failed in this country,' he says. 'The emphasis here is on the quick buck, while the emphasis in Japan is to plan decades ahead. The next quarterly dividend is not as important as existence of the company five, 10 or 20 years from now. One requirement for innovation is faith that there will be a future.'"

I had read many times an article that Dr. Deming called "What Happened in Japan?" and had passed around dozens of copies during the time I was with the Science Center of Rockwell International. In addition, I had gotten peripherally involved then with injecting some aspects of the principles pointed out therein into the quality control process at a couple of Rockwell commercial-products plants. After exposure to Dr. Deming's recent grim forecast, I felt I should be newly galvanized into action; but I lacked direction.

I looked around for a special section of the July 20, 1981 issue of *Business Week* devoted to the "current economic, financial and industrial situation in Japan." It had been sent to me several months earlier by Frank Stanton, CBS's former president, whom I met at Harvard at a meeting of a National Academy of Sciences committee. He had brought up the Deming philosophy then, and had remarked that Dr. Deming wasn't getting the recognition he deserved. But the situation was definitely beginning to change. On page 30 of the *Business Week* special section that he had sent was a full page ad for Sumitomo metals, with a large, shiny, metallic-colored reproduction of the Deming Prize. Above this was a headline that proclaimed, "The most famous name in Japanese quality control is American." The text for the ad read:

"His name is Dr. W. Edwards Deming, and he's a quality control expert.

"In 1950, the Union of Japanese Scientists and Engineers (J.U.S.E.) invited Dr. Deming to lecture several times in Japan, events that turned out to be overwhelmingly successful.

"To commemorate Dr. Deming's visit and to further Japan's development of quality control, J.U.S.E. shortly thereafter established the Deming prizes to be presented each year to the Japanese companies with the most outstanding achievements in quality control.

"Today, Dr. Deming's name is well known within Japan's industrial community, and companies compete fiercely to win the prestigious Demings."

A few days passed, and I saw this ad again in a 1981 issue of *Fortune* magazine. And a few weeks later, an ad for Ricoh copiers showing the medal, appeared on a billboard near Los Angeles' International Airport.

I searched at the UCLA research library for other publications that would discuss the Deming phenomenon. I found a couple of items from the *New York Times*, one of which called Dr. Deming "an unadulterated superstar." Still, the most impressive one was from the February, 1981 issue of *Nation's Business*. It had a lot to say about the opinion of William Conway, then Chief Executive Officer of the Nashua Corporation, one of the Fortune 500.

"So enthusiastic about Deming is Nashua's chairman and president, William E. Conway, that he frequently refers to him as 'the founder of the third wave of the Industrial Revolution.'

"The first wave, Conway explains, was the widespread mechanization that began with British textile factories in the 18th century and spread to the U.S. with such machines as the cotton gin. The second, he says, began in the U.S. early in this century with the advent of industrial engineering principles—'what Henry Ford initiated with the Model T'—that meant reducing a job to the simplest functions, applying efficiency programs and producing in mass.

"Adds Conway: 'There is no doubt in my mind that this whole use of statistical analysis to solve the problems of production and service is the third wave.'"

By the time I finished reading this article, I had been home from Washington for about a week, but the events of the trip were still fresh in my mind. Its purpose was to attend, as a newly elected vice president, a two-day meeting of the board of directors of the American Statistical Association (ASA), preceded by a one-day meeting of the Executive Committee of the Board.

On the evening following the first day of the Board meeting, I attended a working dinner, a meeting of the Future Goals Committee of ASA. In attendance were all the ASA officers, including Martin Wilk, who had recently taken early retirement as Director of Corporate Planning for A.T.&T. and subsequently had taken on the job of Chief Statistician of Canada in time to direct their census. As the senior (third-year) ASA vice-president, he had inherited the job of chairing the Future Goals Committee. His agenda for the meeting of the committee touched on several subjects, but the topic of the evening turned out to be, without question, the public understanding of the discipline of Statistics.

Statistical analysis of data is a tool that is often able to unravel mysteries that might otherwise remain unsolved. The profession of statistics is made up of the theorists who use various mathematical techniques to develop the methodologies that make the tool more effective, as well as the applied statisticians who use the tool. Partly because the theoretical foundations of statistical methodologies are not easily explained, it's difficult to communicate to more than a few the criticality that statistical analysis be done by a professional.

When CBS, or NBC, or ABC repeatedly gives a correct projection for the winner of an election half an hour after returns have begun to come in, the public tends to think of this as something "computerization" has achieved. But computerization does not do that by itself. Without the correct application of statistical theory, this amazing feat would be impossible.

About the end of February, a few weeks after our meetings in Washington, Martin Wilk wrote, asking that the committee members send him ideas for improving the public understanding of Statistics. My letter in response reflected thoughts that occurred to me before I left Washington. I suggested that someone should write a book with examples of statistical analysis that are exciting or ingenious or fun, or any combination of these qualities. I felt that such a book, written with care and imagination and properly publicized, could make an impact on the public.

As soon as I had written the letter, I began to think about Dr. Deming. It occurred to me that ASA should give an annual Deming Prize to American industrial firms, just as the J.U.S.E. gives the awards in Japan. I reasoned that the President of the U.S. would be the one who ought to present at least the first such award. After all, the Emperor of Japan has been involved in the Deming Prize activities, as I had seen in Dr. Deming's photo scrapbook. In Japan, the annual award ceremony is broadcast on national television, just like our Academy Awards festivities.

I set down all of these thoughts in a second letter to Martin Wilk, adding that I felt someone should write a book about Dr. Deming and about what happened in Japan and what's now happening in the U.S. on the productivity front.

It may have been the next day, or several days later, that I was suddenly struck with the thought that I wanted to write that book. So, I waited until the next Saturday, when I knew Dr. Deming would be home temporarily from his consulting and lecture circuit, and phoned to tell him the news, namely that I was planning to write a book about him. He liked my news, and we made arrangements to meet a few Saturdays later when he would be again in Washington and I would be there for a meeting of an advisory committee to the Office of Nuclear Regulatory Research.

That Saturday we talked and talked, and somehow my feelings about the undertaking changed. At first, writing the book seemed to be a venture that could perhaps make a contribution to the statistical profession and also tell what I felt was an interesting story. But as Dr. Deming and I talked that Saturday in his office, then in his home and still later over dinner at the Cosmos Club, I began to feel a sense of urgency. I realized that we are indeed in a new economic age, that the public needs to understand what we will be facing if we—American business and industry and all of us—do not adjust to the changes ordained by this new age.

When people are faced by a crisis that comes upon them suddenly, they spring into action quickly, even if the action is not the right one for the moment. But a crisis that develops slowly catches its victims napping. This is the kind of crisis the U.S. is now facing, a trade imbalance that in 1982 was $40 billion and by 1984 has grown to an annual figure of $130 billion. We may yet be able to cope with this crisis if we understand and incorporate the philosophy that has brought about such drastic changes in Japan, so that our economy is not reduced to an unacceptably low level.

I realize that to say Western civilization is at a crossroad is a strong statement to make; but it may well be the only conclusion left for any thinking person when the low quality of Western production and the sad state of Western productivity is compared with that of the country, that after being totally destroyed, has totally subscribed to the Deming philosophy of excellence.

CONTENTS

CHAPTER 1

**WHY IT HAPPENED IN JAPAN
AND NOT IN THE U.S.**

"We are in a new economic age. We can no longer live with commonly accepted levels of delays, mistakes, defective materials and defective workmanship."

I first heard these words from W. Edwards Deming a little over a year after I had met this remarkable man. At that time I was developing statistical methods for the analysis of reliability data at the Research Division of Rocketdyne, where rocket engines were being produced for the Apollo moon program. Nearly everyone with whom I've spoken since I first began to write and give talks about Deming-related topics has asked me how I happen to know him. So, I'll begin this chapter with our initial encounter. The event, which was something of an aborted disaster, took place in 1968 when he was in his 68th year.

Dr. Deming was then a consultant for several large corporations, carriers of motor freight, railroads, telephone companies and the like, as he still is, and in this capacity he had attained some prominence as an expert court witness. In addition, he was a Professor in the Graduate School of Business Administration at New York University, though his principal residence was and still is in Washington, D.C. It was both his "expert witness" status and his N.Y.U. affiliation (still as active as ever, but as an Emeritus appointment since 1975) that led to our first conversation.

Early in 1968, I was helping to put together a conference,

Computer Science and Statistics: A Symposium on the Interface, for which the organizing committee had decided to have a session on "Jurimetrics," statistical aspects of court proceedings or the treatment of statistical problems in court. Another committee member, Elizabeth King, had taken some graduate courses with Professor Deming some years earlier when she had worked for A.T.&T. in New York. At her suggestion, we invited him to come to Los Angeles and give a Jurimetrics paper at our meeting. He accepted and arranged to adjust his schedule so that his visit to Los Angeles would follow a consulting trip to San Francisco. As a result, there was to be little or no cost to the conference for his travel expenses. This was fortunate since our budget then could euphemistically be described as zero-based.

All was well until we sent Dr. Deming a copy of the conference brochure, which listed him as "W. Edwards Deming, New York University." Upon reading this, he phoned Elizabeth to tell her that he liked to be given credit as someone who was able to make a good living as a "Consultant in Statistical Studies" (the title that now appears on his letterhead), and that he therefore had decided not to come to our meeting and give the talk.

The job of calling him to apologize fell to me for two reasons. First, I was the one who was responsible for the nearly fatal error; and second, I was chairman of the conference (the old "buck stops here" syndrome). As it turned out, only a few seconds of apology were necessary; he conferred instant absolution as soon as I claimed responsibility for the gaffe. He came to Los Angeles as planned and helped to make the conference a resounding success. It became the second annual get-together of a series of meetings that continues to be organized and held at places like Harvard, the U.S. Bureau of Standards, the University of Waterloo in Canada, etc.

The first time I saw Dr. Deming after Interface II was about a year later. In the meantime he had been mugged one night in Greenwich Village, while walking from the apartment he kept there, close to N.Y.U. and his New York clients, to mail a letter. The mugger had asked for his wallet and when this determined "consultant in statistical studies" had refused to give it to him, the man had slipped a knife between his ribs, puncturing a lung. As a result, Dr. Deming had reluctantly allowed his family to talk him into moving to a safer part of Greenwich Village after his recovery.

When we met in May of 1969, seven months after the mugging, he was healthy and robust. In fact, following a cocktail party at his new New York apartment one evening, a dozen or so of us had trouble keeping up with him as we walked to a nearby restaurant for dinner. The reason for our May meeting was the first international conference at which I was invited to speak. And was it held in Montevideo or Venice, or even London? No, it was in Washington, a city I had visited for various reasons several times that year. Nonetheless, it was nice to be invited.

Some time before the conference, I received an invitation to join Dr. Deming and another conference speaker for dinner at the Cosmos Club on the first evening of the event. I accepted, and then upon my arrival in town, touched base by phone to find when I should meet them for the occasion. It was then that I discovered that the other speaker was unable to join us.

That left the two of us to eat and talk, once we met in the Ladies' Parlor, just inside the ladies' entrance to the Cosmos Club. (In those days, my consciousness of male chauvinism was languishing comfortably, yet to be raised, so I paid little attention to this quaint arrangement.) Mealtime provided a chance for me to find out how Dr. Deming, who was originally trained in physics and mathematics, had made such an impact on the discipline of statistical quality control and had had so much influence in its being applied in this country and in Japan.

Recently, I have refreshed my memory and filled in details in conversations with Dr. Deming on several Saturday and Sunday afternoons we spent in his office in Washington between his trips to British Columbia, The Netherlands, Japan, Korea and most of the major, and many of the minor, cities of the United States.

The story should begin in March of 1938, ten years after Dr. Deming earned his Ph.D. in physics at Yale and shortly before he left his position as a mathematical physicist at the U.S. Department of Agriculture (USDA) to join the U.S. Bureau of the Census. At the time, he arranged for Dr. Walter Shewhart, the father of process control, to deliver a series of four lectures entitled "Statistical Method from the Viewpoint of Quality Control" at the USDA Graduate School, where Dr. Deming had charge of courses in mathematics and statistics. Dr. Shewhart was based in New York City at the Bell Telephone Laboratories where he and Dr. Deming had met some years earlier. Working together, the two became fast friends. Dr. Shewhart's lectures at the USDA were published by the Graduate School in 1939 "with the editorial assistance of W. Edwards Deming."

Shewhart, in his 1931 book, "Economic Control of Quality of Manufactured Product," had given his criteria for determining when numerical data are in statistical control. Shewhart demonstrated brilliance in realizing that potential information is generated by all industrial processes, and he developed simple methods whereby one can chart sequentially averages of measurements of, for example, the diameter of a metal disk being turned out by a particular manufacturing process. One can thereby create a series of pictures that show fluctuations in the process and can then use the pictures as a tool to determine when the system is out of statistical control and exhibiting more than simple random variation. One of the uses of this kind of feedback is in identifying local sources of trouble, such as, for example, individual workers who may, perhaps, need more training or particular machines or times of week.

An important part of Shewhart's contribution is that local sources of trouble must be eliminated, allowing a process to remain in statistical control, before innovations leading to improved productivity can be achieved. When there are inordinately large deviations from normal operations of a system because of the unexplained local causes, it is impossible to evaluate the effects of changes in design, training, purchasing policy, etc., made in the system by management. This implication and, in fact, the whole concept of statistical process control made a profound impact on W. Edwards Deming.

Dr. Joseph Juran, a consultant in management methods, estimated in the early fifties that about 15 percent of the problems in an organization are due to local causes that could be changed by the workers. This leaves management with the responsibility for 85 percent of potential improvement through changes in the system. Very often workers, if asked, can identify problems that cause inefficiencies; but only management can change the process. Or, as Dr. Deming puts it, "When a worker gets his output into statistical control, he can do no more."

A point not to be missed is that if a process is in control, there are no local sources of problems. In this state, study of defectives yields no useful information for improvement. The control chart, however, can reveal whether the average value being turned out is higher or lower than desired, how much variability is exhibited by the process, and whether the data show trends or any other sort of non-random behavior. Study of inputs to the process, materials for example, or of the process itself, can then usually allow one to identify the source of the difficulties and make corrections, a first step in fine-tuning the system.

Shewhart was concerned with the application of his methods and techniques for controlling the quality of industrial production processes, as he showed in his 1931 and 1939 books. Just as Dr. Shewhart exhibited creativity in developing control methodology based on statistical variations in processes, Dr. Deming showed profound insight in realizing the tremendous potential of this and other statistical aids for continuous improvement of a production process and the delivery of a quality product, whatever it might be. He discovered that the methods apply equally well to banks, department stores, railways, the mail and other service industries, uses for statistical process control that were not anticipated by Dr. Shewhart.

Dr. Deming began work at the Bureau of the Census, and it occurred to him that quality control procedures could be applied to the routine clerical operations of the 1940 population census, such as coding and card-punching. During the learning period, the error rate of an individual punching cards was high; but with training and experience, a good card puncher's error rate dropped markedly and could be brought under statistical control. At first, the work of all card punchers received 100% verification or correction; later nearly 40% qualified for only sample verification.

Work subject only to sample proofing flowed through the process six times faster than otherwise. Deming and Leon Geoffrey, in an article in the September 1941 issue of the *Journal of the American Statistical Association,* estimated that the introduction of quality control saved the ‚Bureau several hundred thousand dollars, which were transferred to other work and also, above all, contributed to earlier publication of census results. Use of statistical quality control procedures has been a standard practice at the Bureau of the Census ever since.

The next relevant series of events began early in 1942, soon after World War II had broken out. Dr. Deming, who was then working at the Bureau of the Census and was also a consultant to the Secretary of War, received a letter from W. Allan Wallis. Wallis, who later became Undersecretary of State for Economic Affairs, was at that time on the Statistics faculty of Stanford University and concerned that Stanford seemed to be relatively untouched by events in the world outside the campus. He and several other members of Stanford's Statistics faculty were seeking guidance on how they might contribute to the war effort.

Dr. Deming responded to Wallis's letter with four single-spaced pages on the letterhead of the Chief of Ordnance. After some explanatory background on the theme that, "the only useful function of a statistician is to make predictions, and thus to provide a basis for action," he wrote:

> "Here is my idea. Time and materials are at a premium, and there is no time to be lost. There is no royal short cut to producing a highly trained statistician, but I do firmly believe that the most important principles of application can be expounded in a very short time to engineers and others. I have done it and have seen it done. You could accomplish a great deal by holding a school in the

Shewhart methods some time in the near future. I would suggest a concentrated effort—a short course followed by a long course. The short course would be a two-day session for executives and industrial people who want to find out some of the main principles and advantages of a statistical program in industry. It would be a sort of popularization, four lectures by noted industrial people who have seen statistical methods used and can point out some of their advantages. The long course would extend over a period of weeks, or, if given evenings, over a longer period. It would be attended by the people who actually intend to use statistical methods on the job. In many cases they would be delegated by the men who had attended the short course.

"I would suggest that both courses be thrown open to engineers, inspectors, and industrial people with or without mathematical and statistical training. . . ."

On the first of May, Wallis wrote Deming that though his letter had arrived only a few hours earlier, the ideas he presented had struck home so well that plans for proceeding with them were already under way. A mere three weeks later, the first letter about the quality control course to be offered at Stanford went to firms supplying Army ordnance in the Western United States; and the first course was given in July of 1942.

Stanford's Holbrook Working, writing in *Science,* November, 1942, described how the Deming inspiration was put into action. Suitable machinery for organizing the suggested course was already in existence in the engineering science and management War Training Program; and so was financing, through the Office of Education.

10

With the aid of active support from the Ordnance Department, through its San Francisco District Office, 29 key men were brought together only a few weeks after the original suggestion had been received. These men, from industries holding war contracts and from procurement agencies of various branches of the armed services, took an intensive ten-day course with classes running eight hours a day. All 29, plus Professors Working and Eugene Grant of Stanford, completed the course. Two months later in Los Angeles, it was given again under Stanford's auspices. The instructors were Deming and Ralph Wareham of the General Electric Company, as well as Charles Mummery of the Hoover Company. Mr. Mummery had learned the Shewhart methods through self study, and Mr. Wareham had studied statistical theory at the University of Iowa.

The project was such a success that, beginning early in 1943, intensive 8-day courses in statistical quality control were given at many universities throughout the country under the auspices of the U.S. Office of Education. Dr. Deming was the teacher of 23 of them. Within two years, the courses had been attended by almost 2000 men and women from nearly 700 industrial concerns. Many of the students went on to serve as instructors in part-time courses in which another 31,000 persons in industry participated.

The program had a strongly beneficial effect on the quality and volume of war production. Spectacular reductions in scrap and rework were made. But process control was used mostly as a tool for dealing with local crises.

The wartime experience helped lay the groundwork for the establishment of the American Society for Quality Control (ASQC) in February 1946. Dr. Deming, who played an important role in the founding of this society, told me:

"Wherever I taught, I told the people, 'Nothing will happen if you don't keep working together. And you've learned only a little, so you must keep on working and meeting together.' They did, and out of that nucleus grew the ASQC."

The ASQC showed its appreciation to Dr. Deming by giving him in 1956 its most prestigious award, the Shewhart Medal.

It was in a 1981 *Military Science and Technology* interview that Dr. Deming gave the principal reason that statistical quality control methodology did not substantially increase competitive position in this country, though it had succeeded so brilliantly in Japan:

"The courses were well received by engineers, but management paid no attention to them. Management did not understand that they had to get behind improvement of quality and carry out their obligations from the top down."

In several conversations that I had with Dr. Deming in 1982, he expanded on this theme by discussing the random variation that defines a process:

"In the wartime courses we taught people that there is variation in all things and that the measurements that one takes from a manufacturing process must exhibit stability, or they don't have any meaning as far as defining the process. Any instabilities can help to point out specific times or locations of local problems. Once these local problems are removed, there is a process that will continue until somebody changes it. It might be a change in chemistry, a change in temperature or pressure. It would require study by engineers, chemists and people who understand, after a fashion, the production process. Changing the process is management's responsibility. And we failed to teach them that.''

So it was that methodology for improvement of quality began to evolve in the United States but failed to realize its potential. If things had been a bit different, it might have been the U.S.A. that experienced a quality Renaissance. Conditions were right in many ways, but there was a missing essential ingredient, namely management's awareness that there was a growing problem and that there was a means of dealing with it.

For the most part, quality assurance in the U.S. has come to mean sampling inspection, often government ordained, which is done after the level of quality is built into a product. Christopher S. Gray, in a *Business Week* article entitled "Total Quality Control in Japan — Less Inspection, Lower Cost," quotes Hidetaro Mori of Toshiba's Productivity and Industrial Engineering Division: "Even if you inspect every product, you still can't guarantee quality that isn't there." And, of course, the waste — from rework, scrap and increased service calls and the ill will and bad publicity that result from a failure to build quality into the product by means of process control — plays havoc with competitive position.

There have been over the years in the U.S. quality-assurance managers and engineers who have used control charts and other statistical devices to monitor manufacturing processes or other production systems. Until recently they were not generally looked upon by higher management as individuals whose knowledge and experience could materially enhance the productivity of the company. Instead, quality assurance tended to rank in prestige near the bottom of a list that was headed by sales and other areas more closely connected with short-term profits. Management in most companies did not see the connection between quality and competitive position and did not see a need to take responsibility for putting process control and quality assurance to work. They did not understand that statistical methods can be used as a tool to identify problems and to fine-tune systems.

In Japan, it was a totally different story. There, upper management did grasp the fact that building quality into a product results in an increase in competitive position and did see to it that statistical quality assurance methods were incorporated in their production schemes. The saga of how that happened began in 1946 when Dr. Deming made a trip around the world under the auspices of the Economic and Scientific Section of the U.S. Department of War. While he was in India working with Mahalanobis, the Indian statistician who had founded the Indian Statistical Institute, he received instructions to continue on to Japan. He did so and stayed there for two months to assist U.S. occupation forces with studies of nutrition, agricultural production, housing, fisheries, etc. Thus, he became friends with some of the great Japanese statisticians. Statistics as a profession was well established there.

Dr. Deming does not know why there were so many learned statisticians in Japan those many years ago. He remembers, however, that one or two young Japanese had been studying statistics at University College in London when he had taken classes there a few years earlier. He and the Japanese went there to learn from Sir Ronald Fisher, regarded by many as the father of modern statistics. Dr. Deming reminisced to me about his experiences with the Japanese statisticians during the post-war years.

"In 1948, I went again to Japan, this time for the Department of Defense, to do more of what I had done before. I talked whenever possible with Japanese statisticians. I would buy food at the Post Exchange, where I had privileges, and lug it to my room at the Army operated Dai-Ichi Hotel. Then I would arrange for a private dining room in the hotel and serve the food to my Japanese friends.

"Any food tasted good to them, I'm sure. We'd sit around the table and talk. I had no vision of what was to happen. I just told them that they were important to the country in the reconstruction of Japan. This idea was new to them.

"Now, there is a sub-plot involving a Mr. Ken-ichi Koyanagi, who had earlier been incarcerated for 8 years — ostensibly for being a Communist. Whether he had been under house arrest or actually in jail, I don't know. Probably all there was to it was that he had a mind of his own and wouldn't go along with the war lords. I say this because when it came time for him to get a visa to come to this country, there was no great problem.

"His major at the university was German literature. Most people who rise in management in Japan never have studied Management Science, thank goodness. It's better that they don't. In 1946, Mr. Koyanagi formed the Union of Japanese Scientists and Engineers (J.U.S.E.) consisting then of 7 engineers, their purpose being the reconstruction of Japan.

"Mr. Koyanagi held the group together. And Dr. Nishibori, who was in the original group and later Chairman of Japan's equivalent of our Atomic Energy Commission, told me that they had nothing much to talk about. They would just eat and drink. Suddenly one night, Dr. Nishibori had the bright idea that statistical methods could help in the reconstruction of Japan. This would be a way of helping that wouldn't require new equipment, which they had no means of obtaining."

During his many visits to Japan, Dr. Deming often had opportunities to get together with some of the original members of J.U.S.E. Dr. Nishibori, on one such occasion, confirmed that it was Dr. Deming's earlier encouragement that had precipitated his suggestion about using statistical methods to help with the rebuilding of Japan. One of the principal problems of Japanese industry had been that the captive markets of China and Korea they had had before the war were now lost to them. And they needed to trade so that they could import food.

In late 1949, Dr. Deming received a letter from Mr. Koyanagi asking him to come to Japan to teach statistical methods for industry. Although he could not go immediately because he had too many projects underway, he did finally make the trip in June of 1950 under the auspices of the Supreme Commander of the Allied Powers.

On November 10, 1965, *The Mainichi Daily News,* a Tokyo newspaper devoted to commerce and business, described the visit and conditions in Japan immediately following the war. The English language version of the article is reproduced in a little diary, a sort of combination journal and scrapbook called "My Seventh Trip to Japan" by W. Edwards Deming, "Unexpurgated, unmeditated, unimaginative. Being a candid day-by-day account of the incredible experiences of a weary statistician, working in Japan, in continued admiration and amazement at

16

the ability of the Japanese people to be so charming along with their dazzling attainments. Typed from original notes written on the spot. Illustrated with the author's own snapshots." The newspaper article noted that in 1950 few Japanese realized the significance of quality control.

"In the prewar years, there were, indeed, some Japanese scholars and engineers who were engaged in the study of quality control, and some of them attempted to put it into practice. But no company dared to carry out the wholesale introduction of the revolutionary idea.

"After the war, the nation's industry was quick to rise again, but the quality of its products were all but inferior. Faced with enormous demand, manufacturers were all busy in turning out as many products as possible, and no one cared about quality.

"The concept of quality control made inroads into the Japanese industries in the form of an Occupation Forces order to communication equipment manufacturers. When they started to employ the modern production formula, some private organizations paid a deep concern. Soon they stepped into the field and started dissemination activities.

"Independent from these organizations, the J.U.S.E. also launched an educational service of quality control in 1948. A series of lectures was sponsored on the subject of statistical analysis of small samples. Several Japanese experts gathered to form a research group, primarily aimed at collecting necessary literature. But these activities had a discouraging result: there was little experience and material available. Still under occupation, Japan was in no position to obtain enough literature and material related to quality control."

Then came Dr. Deming's acceptance of Mr. Koyanagi's invitation.

> ". . . to the joy and surprise of all the people concerned. In his first lecture meeting in Tokyo in mid-1950, 230 scholars and statisticians gathered, impressed by the exciting concept of statistical quality control uttered by the U.S. scholar. In another lecture meeting in Fukuoka, 110 were present.

> "Dr. Deming called on the students to come out of their studies and, with courage and confidence, go into factories, to keep contact with, and teach, business managers and engineers, and to promote their theoretical research on the application of statistical methods."

Dr. Deming lectured in English, but he had a translator, Mr. Hisamachi Kano, whose talents he describes with great admiration. Mr. Kano's father was a banker, and as a child, the younger Kano lived in New York, London and Paris, learning English and French as he grew up. Dr. Deming recalled with obvious fondness:

> "His English was absolutely perfect, with every kind of idiom. I was very fortunate because I had him with me at all times on every visit over a period of over ten years."

Dr. Deming described to me the fateful events that eventually involved the industrial leaders of Japan in the educational process and provided the critical impetus for changing the image of Japanese products.

"They were wonderful students, but on the first day of the lectures a horrible thought came to me, 'Nothing will happen in Japan; my efforts will come to naught unless I talk to top management.' By that time I had some idea of what top management must do. There are many tasks that only the top people can perform: consumer research, for example, and work with vendors. I knew that I must reach top management. Otherwise it would just be another flop as it had been in the States.

"I do everything the hard way. That's one way to do it. I immediately talked to American friends who knew the right Japanese and before long, I was talking to Mr. Ichiro Ishikawa, who had formed the great Kei-dan-ren, the Japanese association of top management. He was also President of J.U.S.E., which I did not know at the time. I knew Mr. Koyanagi; he was Managing Director and did all the work. The office of President of J.U.S.E. was more or less honorary. All of this would have been so simple if I had only been aware of these facts."

After three sessions with Dr. Deming, Mr. Ishikawa saw what needed to be done. He sent telegrams to the 45 top industrialists, telling them to come to the Industry Club the following Tuesday at 5 o'clock to hear Dr. Deming. They all came. Dr. Deming told me:

"I did the best I could. I gave them encouragement. That was the main thing. I told them that they could produce quality for the Western consumer, industrial and household, and develop international trade for food and equipment.

"They thought that they could not accomplish this

19

because they had such a terrible reputation when it came to quality. But they knew what good quality was. Ask anybody in our Navy, and he will tell you that. What they made for military purposes was superb. But for consumer goods, they'd never tried. They didn't know what it was to stand in back of any goods. At that time a Japanese item wouldn't last very long.''

"I told them, 'Those days are over. You can produce quality. You have a method for doing it. You've learned what quality is. You must carry out consumer research, look toward the future, produce goods that will have a market years from now and stay in business. You have to do it to eat. You can send quality out and get food back. The city of Chicago does it. The people of Chicago do not produce their own food. They make things and ship them out. Switzerland does not produce all its own food, nor does England.'

"Incoming materials were terrible, off gauge and off color, nothing right. And I urged them to work with their vendors and to work on instrumentation. A lot of what I urged them to do came very naturally to the Japanese, though they were not doing it. I said, 'You don't need to receive the junk that comes in. You can never produce quality with that stuff. But with process controls that your engineers are learning about, specifications as loose as possible, consumer research, redesign of products, you can. Don't just make it and try to sell it. Redesign it and then again bring the process under control. The cycle goes on and on continuously, with quality ever increasing.' ''

The Japanese came to call this process of continual redesign based on studying the effects of changes, "the Deming cycle," though Dr. Deming credits his old friend Shewhart. It was an essential ingredient in the founding of Japan's industrial revolution.

After Dr. Deming talked more about the problems of manufacturing quality products and how he made the Japanese understand them, he explained to me how he had come to understand them himself.

"I knew the problems because I'd been at Aberdeen Proving Ground, working there for the War Department, with people in industry. And look at the Bureau of the Census. It was one of the largest organizations to use process control to improve quality and productivity.

"One of the big problems of management is to define quality and realize that there are several facets. One is what you're trying to do for the future, whatever quality you're aiming at. Should your purchasing agent continue to buy this kind of paint, or should he switch? But also, how about turning out product today? What is the plant manager's job today?

"Now only management can work on that problem of defining quality. It's a complicated problem with no easy solutions, but it's management's responsibility.

"I tried to explain these things to them, and apparently they understood. They wanted more conferences, so we had more. It was a terrifying experience for me because I was new at it. I was a technical man."

He told them that they would capture markets the world

over within five years. They beat that prediction. Within four years, buyers all over the world were eager to purchase Japanese products.

"I was back in Japan in 6 months, in January of 1951. They already had had many brilliant successes, brilliant fires, just as we had had in the U.S. during the war. But that's not quality; those are just dividends. The top management showed me what they were doing. Mr. Nishimura, President of the Furukawa Electric Company, was himself working to improve the process that produced insulated wire, cable and other products. He brought control charts to show me, and he was able to reduce the amount of rework to 10% of what it had been.

"Mr. Tanabe, President of the Tanabe Pharmaceutical Company, was himself working on quality control. In a few months he succeeded in producing three times as much para-aminosalicylic acid as before, with the same machinery, by just improving the process.

"But you cannot improve the process until you've achieved statistical control. Then engineers and chemists can see that it will stay this way until they make some changes.

"Now, here were these members of top management showing me what they had done. Six months after that trip, I was there again, and again a year later. They were working hard, and they were getting results. I made it clear to them in those first conferences that this must be company wide. 'Everybody in the company has a job to do to improve quality. And as you improve quality, your productivity will go up. You will have something to sell and your customers will be happy.'

"I also told them 'This movement must be nation-wide. You must teach other companies, teach your competitors, move along together. As you learn, tell others.' I didn't have to tell them that. That was the natural Japanese way of working. But I did tell them anyway."

By the time Dr. Deming had made several trips to Japan, J.U.S.E. was able to teach hundreds. They had courses for people outside Tokyo in the daytime and courses in Tokyo in the evening for people who were working there during the day. There were also courses for management. Between 1950 and 1960, they trained 20,000 in rudimentary statistical methods. The courses for management are today booked up seven months ahead.

In 1951, J.U.S.E. established the Deming Prizes, financed originally from the royalties of a book, "Elementary Principles of the Statistical Control of Quality," which J.U.S.E. published from Dr. Deming's lecture notes. The awarding of the prizes is now an annual affair. The prize for research and education is given to individuals, and the "Application Prize" goes to corporations or plants that have demonstrated outstanding results in improvement of quality. Today, a total of four application prizes are given, one for large corporations, two for smaller enterprises and one for factories or divisions.

In each case, the award is a silver medal bearing an engraved profile of Dr. Deming. The Deming Prize Committee, appointed by J.U.S.E., selects the winners. Candidates for the application prizes must have demonstrated methods for improvement of quality as well as success in application. Management needs a good five years before they can even hope to become eligible to win via organization-wide education and testing.

The September, 1954 issue of *Industrial Quality Control* contains an article by Mr. Koyanagi about the second awarding of the Deming Prizes in 1952. In it are observations of Keizo Nishimura, President of Furukawa Electric Company, the recipient of the 1952 Deming Application Prize. Mr. Nishimura, whose dramatic successes with statistical process control were described by Dr. Deming, relates, "I confess that it was not without skepticism that I first listened to Dr. Deming's assertion that quality control is the key to the reconstruction of Japanese industries and that its adoption would make an epoch in Japan's industrial history; but now I know it's every inch true."

The rapport W. Edwards Deming had with the Japanese engineers, scientists and managers was underscored in a pamphlet by Kenichi Koyanagi published by J.U.S.E. in 1960 and called "The Deming Prize." On page 8 Koyanagi writes as follows:

> "Most of the Japanese were in a servile spirit as the vanquished, and among Allied personnel there were not a few with an air of importance. In striking contrast, Dr. Deming showed his warm cordiality to every Japanese whom he met and exchanged frank opinions with everybody. His high personality deeply impressed all those who learned from him and became acquainted with him. He loved Japan and the Japanese with his own heart. The sincerity and enthusiasm with which he did his best for his courses still lives and will live forever in the memory of all concerned."

In 1960, in recognition of his monumental contribution, Dr.

Deming was decorated in the name of the Emperor of Japan with the Second Order of the Sacred Treasure.

So, the explanation of why this miracle happened in Japan lies in the coming together of all the necessary factors for a transformation. Japanese industry, after the war, experienced a "bottoming out." W. Edwards Deming came upon the scene and learned to appreciate the Japanese personality and culture. He had an awareness of what needed to be done, and he saw to it that the message was communicated to the people with the ability to take action. The Kei-dan-ren, the organization for Japan's top management, supplied the means for getting the message to all of Japanese industry — and the means for continued co-operation. J.U.S.E. was in place, ready to provide training and facilities. And the Japanese cultural heritage created precisely the national psychology that made product excellence a reality.

After the war, almost all of these factors were missing in the U.S. Here there was no bottoming out, rather a feeling of ebullience and optimism. We thought we could go on forever dominating world markets. Weren't we providing aid all over the world and expanding our economy explosively?

During the war when the U.S. mentality would have been more conducive to receiving a message explaining how to improve productivity and competitive position, there was no one in top industrial management who had ever thought that statistical quality control could become important to the U.S. Besides, no one understood at that time the responsibilities of management. The attitude of working for short-term profits and blaming business failures on fiscal policies and the hourly workers was a deeply ingrained habit. The 1982 book, "Life and Death on the Corporate Battlefield," by Paul Solomon and

Thomas Friedman focuses on corporate America's incessant desire for quick payoffs and its lack of stress on quality of product.

Dr. Deming in 1982 spoke to me of the growing awareness in this country of the results of his work that shook Japan.

> "Now people in this country are beginning to be aware of the miracle and are trying to find out about it, thinking they can copy the Japanese. They cannot. People can't go to Japan and learn because they don't know enough about the subject. They come back and say they didn't see any quality control."

Dr. Lloyd S. Nelson of the Nashua Corporation expanded on this theme during a presentation at the 1982 Annual Meeting of the American Statistical Association. He pointed out that statistical thinking and statistical methods are abstract. They are not tangible like robots. He described a visit of a team from a large American company sent to Japan to find out what it is that they are doing differently. They took hundreds of photographs, which upon their return, were enlarged and studied by experts. There final verdict was that the Japanese don't have anything that we don't have — perhaps slightly newer models of some production equipment, but nothing fundamentally different. Nelson summed up the problem.

> "Statistical thinking and statistical methods don't produce a latent image on photographic film. The searchers looked in the wrong place and used the wrong technique — what better guarantee of failure? And all of this was carried out with the genuine cooperation of the Japanese. However, after you have been using a technique (borrowed from your guests!) for some 30 years, it

would hardly occur to you to mention it as a critical ingredient. It might, to the Oriental way of thinking, be impolite to say so."

CHAPTER 2

TODAY — THE JAPANESE CHALLENGE
AND THE FOURTEEN POINTS

29

"For many years Japanese manufacturers have made a daring attempt to wipe out the reputation of inferior quality and cheap price which their products had built up before World War II. Today they emerge victorious. Japanese merchandise is tremendously popular around the world, not because it is cheap but superior and dependable."

These were the beginning paragraphs of the 1965 article in Tokyo's *Mainichi Daily News,* which was quoted in the preceding chapter. The article continues.

"Behind this success are the fatherly guidance and devotion by a leading American statistician, Dr. W. Edwards Deming, now professor of New York University. In the early postwar years, he opened the eyes of Japanese manufacturers to the modern approach to the quality problem and taught them how to make their products attractive among the world consumers.

"Dr. Deming is now in Tokyo on his seventh visit to Japan. This afternoon, he and Mrs. Deming will be distinguished guests in a grand ceremony at the Imperial Hotel, Tokyo, to fete the 15th anniversary of the establishment of the Deming Prize — the nation's most coveted award given every year to the outstanding contributors to the research and application of statistical quality control which the U.S. scholar had introduced to Japan. . . ."

"The Deming Prize was created in 1951 by the Union of Japanese Scientists and Engineers (J.U.S.E.) to commemorate the friendship and contribution of Dr. Deming to the whole spectrum of Japanese industry. The prize has played a significant role to give an impetus to industry in its dazzling growth.

"Dr. Deming has been an unequalled teacher and consultant to Japanese industry. He has worked together with thousands of Japanese corporate executives, engineers and scholars for the past 15 years. He set the guideline to bring prosperity to this island country burdened with scarce natural resources. What the U.S. scholar showed his Japanese students was the scientific way to turn out more products that have greater uniformity, dependability and marketability all over the world."

The admiration for Dr. Deming reflected in this article and the mood of celebration surrounding the awarding of the prizes that bear his name are still very much apparent in the 1980s. In November, 1982, 11 video cameras recorded the two-hour-long Deming Prize ceremonies organized by J.U.S.E. and held in Tokyo in the auditorium of the headquarters building of the Japanese organization of top management, Kei-dan-ren. On the day of the event, eight pages of Nihon Keizai Shimbun, the Japanese equivalent of our Wall Street Journal, announced the winners of the various prize categories and described their achievements. Dr. Deming, who was in Tokyo for the ceremonies and the attendant activities, was treated by Japanese industrialists like a visiting potentate.

I observed all of this first hand, having flown to Tokyo for the celebration with Dr. Deming, Diana Cahill, his daughter, and Ronald Moen, Pontiac's Director of Statistical Methods. Diana was accompanying her father in place of her mother, who was not able to make the trip; and Ron Moen had been assigned to study training methods the Japanese used to put the Deming philosophy to work. I was there because I had undertaken, early in the year, the writing of this book. Upon our arrival in Tokyo, we were met by Mr. Junji Noguchi, the General Manager of J.U.S.E., who stayed with us during all activities surrounding the Prize ceremonies.

Several days after the ceremonies, we all made a nearly day-long visit to Yokogawa Hewlett Packard (YHP), winner of the 1982 Deming Application Prize for a division. There, more than two thousand hourly workers joined in the celebration with the enthusiasm of dedicated movie fans outside the site of the Academy Awards ceremonies.

The two limousines that delivered our group to YHP stopped for ten minutes enroute so that the arrival at the plant would be synchronized with the scheduled televising of the event. A huge banner over the main entrance of the YHP facility proclaimed "Welcome Dr. William Edwards Deming — November 19, 1982." Several more such banners hung on various walls inside the building.

Ken Sasaoka, the President of YHP, directed us through the manufacturing areas, pointing proudly to the vividly colored control charts and other statistical problem-solving aids that lined the walls. His rapport with the workers, as he talked with them, was fascinating to behold for those of us used to the schism that exists between workers and management in our country. In his later briefing, Mr. Sasaoka told us that since the installation of the Deming methods for the improvement of quality, YHP's defect rate had fallen from 4 parts per 1000 to 3 parts per million and allowed them to become Hewlett Packard's most profitable division.

They had also cut manufacturing costs by 42 percent and inventory by 64 percent. Concurrently, cycle time for research and development was cut by more than a third, productivity almost doubled, and market share improved by a factor of three. (Hewlett-Packard C.E.O. John A. Young boasted about these latter achievements of YHP in an article in the August, 1985 issue of *Quality Progress.*)

During a luncheon in honor of Dr. Deming, YHP executives presented each of us with a framed reproduction of their Deming prize, showing the Deming profile made of the names of the division's more than 2000 employees. Other Deming Prize winners show their pride in different ways. The Rhythm Watch Company, for instance, which makes clocks sold in this country under the names of Bulova and Timex, gave each employee a quartz clock bearing on its face a facsimile of the Deming medal that the company was about to receive.

We visited Rhythm and also spent a good part of one day at the headquarters of another Deming Prize winner, the Kajima Corporation. Kajima is one of Japan's major construction companies, designing and building huge dams and large luxury hotels and office buildings, the New Otani Hotel and the Sumitomo Bank Building in Los Angeles, for example. We were shown a film on how Kajima had overcome the earlier low levels of productivity resulting from the oil crisis of the 1970s by installing "CWQC," or "company-wide quality control." We saw this film less than three days after the Deming Prize ceremonies. Nevertheless, footage of Kajima's president, Rokuro

Ishikawa, accepting the prize and being congratulated by Dr. Deming, was included.

At the J.U.S.E. headquarters I learned that some form of the Deming Prize had been won over the years by the seven largest industrial corporations in Japan: Toyota, Matsushita Electrical Industries (makers of Panasonic, Quasar and Technics products), Nissan Motors, Nippon Steel, Mitsubishi Heavy Industries, Hitachi and Toshiba. To win the prize requires study and hard work in J.U.S.E. courses in quality-assurance methods by management and by a good part of the working force of an entire corporation, division, or factory. Therefore, the impact of the "Demings," as these prizes are sometimes called, has been considerable in the upgrading of Japanese industry.

The Mainichi Daily News had also commented, "It is said that most corporate candidates are spending years in stream-lining and reinforcing their quality control setup under the guidance of specially invited experts before they apply for the prize." *Business Week* made similar observations on July 20, 1981 in a special advertising section on "Japan: Quality Control and Innovation," in which the various yearly winners were listed.

> "Each year the competition grows in intensity, as more and more companies volunteer to undergo the close scrutiny required. For the firm that wins the prize, and those that gain one of the associated awards, however, the rewards are significant, in profits as well as prestige. For other companies, the ceremony is a time for self-reckoning. The innovations in quality control honored in any year usually soon become national norms."

35

The critical role of Dr. Deming in Japan's rise to its present status is beginning to be understood in the United States, as is shown by many articles and editorials in, for example, *Business Week, Time* and *Fortune* and in the *New York Times,* the *Washington Post,* the *Philadelphia Inquirer* and the *Los Angeles Herald Examiner.* And *Nation's Business* (published by the U.S. Chamber of Commerce) headlined a 1981 article about Dr. Deming, "The American Who Remade 'Made in Japan.'"

There was, too, the 1980 hour and a half long NBC-TV *White Paper,* "If Japan Can, Why Can't We?" the last third of which was devoted almost exclusively to Dr. Deming and the application of the Deming Doctrine, his quality-control philosophy, at the Nashua Corporation. William Conway, then Nashua's president, had called Dr. Deming "the founder of the third wave of the industrial revolution" because of the overwhelming response of the Japanese to his introduction of the concept of a commitment to quality and his teaching of quality assurance methodology for making quality production a reality. A response to NBC's question of "Why can't we?" was provided to a readership of 35 million in the title of the July 1984 *Parade* Sunday supplement magazine article about Dr. Deming by Pulitzer prizewinner David Halberstam: "Yes, We Can."

Yet, we hear or read dozens of analyses of the newly found success of Japanese industry which show the analysts to be oblivious to the quality assurance aspects of the phenomenon. Often they attribute the success to the low wage base in Japan, though it no longer exists. Today's salaries, including bonuses, are slightly higher in Japan than in the United States. In fact, doing business in that tiny, crowded island nation, the size and topography of Montana with about half the population of the U.S., is considerably more costly than in this country. Eighty percent of all raw materials, including all petroleum and petroleum products, are imported; and real estate is so expensive that to rent a parking space in Tokyo for a delivery truck can cost several hundreds of dollars per month. The cost of land in downtown Tokyo reaches almost $15,000 per square foot.

Some analysts credit Japan's success largely to management styles that developed naturally out of its unique cultural heritage. They cite, for example, the tendency of the Japanese to identify strongly with their companies, and they point to the natural inclination of the Japanese for teamwork. Both of these are related to the lifetime employment and "promotion by seniority" that are more or less guaranteed. Yet, all of the aspects of the Japanese culture that are credited were present during the years before World War II when "Made in Japan" meant inexpensive, shoddy products with almost immediate obsolescence built in. Naturally, in those pre-war years, Japan was no threat to our markets.

Japan's being nearly burned to the ground during the war encouraged a climate for change; and Dr. Deming, as the Japanese well know, gave their industrial management the ideas and the tools with which to make such a change a dramatic one. Their cultural heritage and the homogeneity of their society certainly were critical ingredients for the needed metamorphosis, because they provided a nurturing environment for the quality-assurance psychology that Dr. Deming introduced and for the methods he taught. The Japanese government co-operated, and J.U.S.E. carried on the training and promoted the quality-control philosophy. The dedication of top management was, of course, another of the important ingredients. Thus, the concepts taught by Dr. Deming to the engineers and top management, along with the Japanese cultural bent for hard work and study, co-operation, teamwork and the attainment of long-term goals, formed a powerful force.

The fundamental precept taught to the Japanese in the 1950s by Dr. Deming is that building quality into a product brings lower costs and hence improvement in productivity and competitive position. This is an idea that the greater part of American management has not been able to understand, mainly because their concept of quality control has tended to be one of sorting out the bad from the good. Also, of course, until rather recently almost insatiable markets have accepted goods of inferior quality. The local competition of almost any U.S. company is turning out products no better, or very little better, than those it makes itself; so there has been no perceptible need to improve. What would we do without the company across town that makes us look good by comparison?

Similar sentiments have been expressed by Dana M. Cound, Vice-President of Diversitech and 1986 President of the American Society for Quality Control (also an old friend from the time we were both at Rockwell, International). In *Quality Progress,* March 1986, Mr. Cound contended that with the exception of a few product areas, the American forte has never in its history been the production of quality products. Rather, the genius of U.S. industry has been the ability to put serviceable products in the hands of people, at a price the masses could afford. He reminds us that when Henry Ford invented the car which still bears his name, automobiles superior to the Ford, though more expensive, were traveling in Europe on roads better than our own. "Our first real industry may have been the timepiece industry," he says. "Yet," he remarks, "no one who knows anything about horology would suggest that American timepieces set any standards of excellence."

It is not difficult to find other examples of our ability to produce, in great volume, products of less than superior quality. Cotton produced in the United States is far inferior to the high-quality cotton that one can purchase from Mexico or Egypt; and American woolen goods, while good, do not measure up to British woolens, which have always had the quality market and commanded the highest prices.

By and large, the hourly worker in the United States has an appreciation, sometimes an unconscious appreciation, that higher quality means less rework, less waste, a satisfied customer and a chance to take pride in one's work. But most American workers, stultified by fear or apathy, long ago gave up trying to communicate these thoughts to their employers. Instead, a major part of the U.S. working force adopted adversarial tactics similar to those of management, building powerful unions that have exacerbated the schism between management and labor and created a vicious circle of combat that put up ever new barriers to quality output.

In the midst of all this negativity, some members of American management have shown an awareness of the fact that an emphasis on quality is a policy that can allow a company to prosper, even under the battle conditions of the early 1980s. We can read about a few companies that provide things that work and last or that deliver effective service in the 1983 book, "In Search of Excellence," by Thomas J. Peters and Robert H. Waterman. The fact that this book was number one on most national non-fiction bestseller lists in 1983, shows the desperation of many in U.S. management for clues to increasing productivity. Still, for most, increasing productivity continues to mean short-term profits via short cuts in production. In fact, a 1984 *Business Week* article illustrated how several companies cited in the Peters and Waterman book had fallen on bad times because they had succumbed to the lure of short-term rewards.

Meanwhile, the Japanese have continued the trend described

in the 1965 *Mainichi Daily News* article, overtaking not only our country in industries we once dominated, but also England, Germany and Switzerland. They now lead the world in the manufacture of motorcycles, watches, cameras, optical instruments, steel, ships, automobiles, pianos, and consumer electronics.

As portended by early postwar events, the phrase "Made in Japan" has now become a hallmark of superior quality. In May of 1982, a New York radio newscast reported that action was being taken against certain Korean firms that were illegally stamping these words on their products. And, as if this weren't ironic enough for American industry, the cover article of the August 9, 1982 issue of *Newsweek* told us that Tokyo is preparing an unprecedented challenge, with enormous stakes, in the high-technology fields of the future. After warning that unless U.S. and European firms rally to the challenge, the prosperity and the jobs that flow from this industrial revolution will almost certainly go to Japan, it quotes Julian Gresser, president of the East Asia Consulting Group: "The technological battle with the Japanese is really an industrial equivalent to the East-West arms race."

Across the bottom of two pages of this *Newsweek* article is a pictorial strip displaying "The Making of a Miracle." It includes the 1964 unveiling of Japan's first "bullet train," the 1970 accession of Nippon Steel to the title of largest steelmaker in the world, Japanese automakers' production of 11 million cars in 1980, overtaking Detroit for the first time, and the winning by Japan in 1981 of 70% of the world market of the 64k Random-Access-Memory computer board.

The author of this article, being another of those analysts who has overlooked the most important ingredient in the Japanese challenge, makes not a single mention of quality assurance and its criticality in the development of these incredible events. The skill of Japanese engineers and technicians and the labor, management and government policies that are based on the Japanese cultural heritage are understandably credited with creating these miracles. But that the quality assurance technology is the very underpinning of the results of the engineers and technicians is not mentioned.

In referring to productivity, the author comments, "The Japanese have pioneered the widespread use of automation, miniaturization and robotics in mass production, and the innovations have kept Japan out in front of the pack in productivity in many industries."

This statement reflects a naivete, pervasive in the U.S., concerning what is required to perfect such processes. At the Ford Corporation's robotics center in Dearborn, Michigan, there are dozens of robots being tested for repeatability, and computer-directed control charts periodically record the deviations from established norms. A good response to those who believe that robots spring full-blown from the designer's drawing board without constant quality control during many stages of production, is provided by Nashua's Dr. Lloyd S. Nelson.

". . . we are beginning to hear about the completely automatic factory run by robots that not only operate the processes, but also repair each other as required.

"Imagine a robot made by an out-of-statistical-control process attempting to repair another robot with parts from an out-of-control process. This might make a wonderful comedy if you were making movies. But if you're trying to produce manufactured goods, you're all through."

From its origins in statistical process control has grown a philosophy for productivity improvement that, during his many years of consulting, Dr. Deming has tried to make U.S. industry understand. Dr. Myron Tribus, former Assistant Secretary of Commerce for Science and Technology and now Director of M.I.T.'s Center for Advanced Engineering Study, recently likened W. Edwards Deming to a passenger on a large sinking ship who knew precisely what to do to prevent the catastrophe, but to whom very few would listen. But, as we have noted earlier, more and more people are beginning to listen carefully to what Dr. Deming has to say.

On September 8, 1980, almost two years before *Newsweek's* warning of Japan's technological challenge, there appeared in *People* magazine an article entitled " 'Made in Japan' is No Joke Now, Thanks to Edward Deming: His New Problem is 'Made in U.S.A.' " This article describes how more and more American firms (both manufacturing and service organizations) are now seeking out Dr. Deming, learning from him what the Japanese learned, and putting to work his philosophy for improving quality and, hence, productivity.

The foundation of this philosophy consists of the basic ideas originally taught to the Japanese in the fifties. The philosophy involves, of course, quality as an underlying primary goal, and, as it exists today, also takes into account the need to eliminate the obstacles that stand in the way of increasing quality and productivity, obstacles that management policies in the U.S. and in many other nations have erected and promulgated.

Dr. Deming has set down 14 cardinal points encapsulating his philosophy. Following are 1985 and 1986 versions of these, showing how communication of the essence of the philosophy is evolving over time. The evolution is accelerated because Dr. Deming experiences a tremendous amount of feedback because of situations that arise in consulting and as a result of discussions with some among the several thousand who attend his seminars each year. If one compares either of the listings given below with the July 1981 *Business Week* article by Dr. Deming detailing a then current version of the 14 points, scant resemblance in organization and phrasing is revealed.

In the 1986 version, one can notice that statistical methods are no longer explicitly called out, but are rather simply implicit in certain of the admonitions. This change reflects Dr. Deming's concern that some organizations will come to believe that their transformation can be brought about by the incorporation of statistical process control alone. Also, one sees, in contrast to earlier versions, explicit mention of management-by-objective and related evils. The underlying basic ideas of the 14 points have not changed for many years, but as the statement of the philosophy is modified, it tends to explain better the concepts involved.

The first listing of the 14 points given here appears on a card that was handed out in February 1985 at a meeting of the San Diego based Deming Users' Group, attended by nearly 400 naval and civilian employees of the U.S. Naval Air Rework Facility at North Island.

1. Create constancy of purpose towards improving products and services, allocating resources to provide for long-range needs rather than short-term profitability.

2. Adopt the new philosophy for economic stability

by refusing to allow commonly accepted levels of delays, mistakes, defective materials and defective workmanship.

3. Cease dependence on mass inspection by requiring statistical evidence of built-in quality in both manufacturing and purchasing functions.

4. Reduce the number of suppliers for the same item by eliminating those that do not qualify with statistical evidence of quality. End the practice of awarding business solely on the basis of price.

5. Search continually for problems in the system to constantly improve processes.

6. Institute modern methods of training to make better use of all employees.

7. Focus supervision on helping people do a better job. Ensure that immediate action is taken on reports of defects, maintenance requirements, poor tools, inadequate operating definitions, or other conditions detrimental to quality.

8. Encourage effective two-way communication and other means to drive out fear throughout the organization and help people work more productively.

9. Break down barriers between departments by encouraging problem solving through teamwork, combining the efforts of people from different areas such as research, design, sales and production.

10. Eliminate the use of numerical goals, posters, and

slogans for the work force that ask for new levels of productivity without providing methods.

11. Use statistical methods for continuing improvement of quality and productivity, and eliminate work standards that prescribe numerical quotas.

12. Remove all barriers that inhibit the worker's right to pride of workmanship.

13. Institute a vigorous program of education and retraining to keep up with changes in materials, methods, product design and machinery.

14. Clearly define top management's permanent commitment to quality and productivity and its obligation to implement all of these principles.

Note in the following more recent version of the 14 points, besides the references to management-by-objective and the lack of explicit mention of statistical methods or statistical evidence, several uses of the word "leadership." This listing appears in a brochure distributed by Quality Enhancement Seminars in Santa Monica, California, advertising late 1986 Deming seminars in Cincinnati, Ohio and Newport Beach, California.

1. Create constancy of purpose toward improvement of product and service, with the aim to become competitive and to stay in business, and to provide jobs.

2. Adopt the new philosophy. We are in a new economic age. Western Management must awaken to the challenge, must learn their responsibilities, and take on leadership for change.

3. Cease dependence on inspection to achieve quality. Eliminate the need for inspection to achieve quality. Eliminate the need for inspection on a mass basis by building quality into the product in the first place.

4. End the practice of awarding business on the basis of price tag. Instead, minimize total cost. Move toward a single supplier for any one item, on a long-term relationship of loyalty and trust.

5. Improve constantly and forever the system of production and service, to improve quality and productivity, and thus constantly to decrease costs.

6. Institute training on the job.

7. Institute leadership (see point 12). The aim of leadership should be to help people and machines and gadgets to do a better job. Leadership of management is in need of overhaul, as well as leadership of production workers.

8. Drive out fear, so that everyone may work effectively for the company.

9. Break down barriers between departments. People in research, design, sales, and production must work as a team, to foresee problems of production and in use that may be encountered with the product or service.

10. Eliminate slogans, exhortations, and targets for the work force asking for zero defects and new levels of productivity.

11a. Eliminate work standards (quotas) on the factory floor. Substitute leadership.

b. Eliminate management by objective. Eliminate management by numbers, numerical goals. Substitute leadership.

12a. Remove barriers that rob the hourly worker of his right to pride of workmanship. The responsibility of supervisors must be changed from sheer numbers to quality.

b. Remove barriers that rob the hourly worker of his right to pride of workmanship. This means, inter alia, abolishment of the annual or merit rating and of management by objective, management by the numbers.

13. Institute a vigorous program of education and self-improvement.

14. Put everybody in the company to work to accomplish the transformation. The transformation is everybody's job.

It was Dr. Deming's experience at the U.S. Census Bureau, at Aberdeen Proving Ground during World War II and in Japan that shaped this basic philosophy for improving quality and productivity sometime in 1950. While the essentials have changed very little in the course of time since then, specific points have been added and/or refined. There are two fundamental ideas supporting the Deming Doctrine. The first is that management must strive to develop business over the long, the very long term; it is not enough for a business to make a quick profit today. The second is that this goal can be attained only by the delivery of high quality, dependable products and/ or services.

Few would, in theory, question this second precept. Yet one can't help but notice that if turning out superior products and services is, in fact, a goal of American industry, something has been lost in translation to reality.

We all are busy making mistakes, and most of us agree that that's what gives us the greatest potential for learning. The problem seems to be that we aren't making use of this potential and profiting from our mistakes. In Dr. Deming's philosophy, statistical data-analysis techniques are used as mechanisms for tapping and exploiting the potential information generated by the processes turning out goods and services — to anticipate, identify and correct mistakes and thereby reduce variability in the system, improving quality and achieving excellence. Along with improved quality attained by these means are the added dividends of decreased costs through the better use of human effort, machine time and materials and the decrease in rework and scrap. Productivity is thereby increased, markets are captured and ensured over the long term and jobs are provided.

The philosophy is built around the "Deming Cycle," as the Japanese call it. This cycle that Dr. Deming described to them in 1950 uses testing and statistical feedback at various stages of manufacturing and marketing in order constantly to improve a system which involves design, production, merchandising and service. The Deming philosophy, through the Deming Cycle, shows us a way of doing business based on the realization that the customer and the level of customer satisfaction are the most critical elements in the entire production process. The days of, "You can have any color, as long as it's black," are over. In the Deming Doctrine, customers are those who buy the product and also those involved in succeeding stages of production.

Besides working towards customer satisfaction, Dr. Deming emphasizes the importance of satisfaction of the worker and of management, including the elimination of adversarial positions. The major, overall goal is productivity through efficiency and delivery of a product in which workers and management can take pride and which consumers will buy because they believe in it.

A February, 1982 article in *American Business* describes "constancy of purpose" as the cornerstone of the Deming philosophy. In one sense this is true, since constancy of purpose embodies the ideas that make up the philosophy's foundation, i.e., constant improvement of product and service to guarantee the future of the business. But the use of statistical methods of quality control is of equal importance. It is the glue that holds everything together.

It is not enough, though, to install statistical methods, as has been done in some U.S. companies; it is necessary to provide every employee with the required understanding of these methods. It also means making use of the results throughout a company for never-ending improvement of the product or service, something hardly ever done in this country. Implementation, however, requires a recognition of the barriers (management failures) that stand in the way of increasing quality and productivity. These must be eliminated before statistical methods can be introduced.

In a 1986 keynote address presented at an international meeting in Australia of The Institute of Management Science (TIMS) and the Operations Research Society of America (ORSA), Dr. Deming spoke of some of these barriers and some of the misconceptions of self-styled experts about requirements for improvement of quality and productivity.

> "The biggest problem that most any company in the Western world faces is not its competitors, nor the Japanese. The biggest problems are self-inflicted, created right at home by management that are off course in the competitive world of today."

Systems of management in place in the Western world, he said, are such that survival demands that they be blasted out and new construction commenced. "Patchwork will not suffice."

> "There is much talk about the need to improve quality and productivity. Moreover, everyone knows exactly how to go about it.

> "In the eyes of many people in management the big trouble is that a lot of employees in operations, and in management as well, are careless and neglectful on the job. One writer has the solution — hold all employees accountable for job behavior as well as for the results expected of them. The fact is that performance appraisal, management by the numbers, management by objective and work standards have already devastated Western industry. More of the same could hardly be a solution.

> "Other writers see information as the solution. Anyone can improve his work, they say, if he has enough information. The fact is that a figure by itself provides no information, has no meaning, no interpretation, in the absence of theory. In short, there is no substitute for knowledge; and a figure by itself is not knowledge.

"Other people put their faith in gadgets, computers, new machinery, and robotic machinery. Solving problems is not the answer, nor improvement of operations. They are not the transformation required.

"It will not suffice to match the competition. He that declares his intention to meet the competition is already licked, his back to the wall. Likewise, zero defects are a highway down the tube. The sad truth is that all the parts of an apparatus may meet the specifications, and yet the apparatus may be unsatisfactory or may even be a total failure. It is necessary in this world to outdo specifications, to move continually toward better and better performance of the finished product."

Although Dr. Deming did not explicitly mention his 14-point philosophy in this TIMS/ORSA address, it is clear that the 14 points hold the keys to what Western management so desperately needs.

The 14 points can be organized in different ways. They may fall into categories having to do with internal use of statistical techniques, with labor-management relations, supplier-management relations, and overall management philosophy. Chapters 3, 4, 5, and 6 treat these different concepts.

All of the 14 points are somewhat overlapping and are very much interdependent. Improvement in one area facilitates improvement in another, and ignoring any one of the points causes problems in making the philosophy work.

As a result of adopting the Deming 14 points, Pontiac has reorganized its entire management structure to provide means of implementing the doctrine and to monitor constantly the effectiveness of this implementation. It is an ongoing process that has involved nearly every one of the division's more than 12,000 employees. During a two-day visit there in 1982, about two years before the 1984 reorganization of General Motors, I heard people from all levels call out specific points of Dr. Deming's 14, by number, showing the importance they all attach to them. The film "Roadmap for Change — The Deming Approach," made by the Encyclopedia Britannica Educational Corporation, shows how Pontiac's drastic change of management style allowed them to "improve quality and increase productivity" in building their Fiero model, new and highly acclaimed in 1983.

Pontiac has its own version of the 14 points resulting from a directed effort to capture their essence during a two-day off-site meeting of the senior and assistant staff, called by General Manager Bill Hoglund. This policy statement, "The Pontiac Quality Philosophy," which I found framed and hanging on the walls of several offices at Pontiac headquarters, reads as follows.

"Pontiac Motor Division commits itself to quality as our number one business objective. We are dedicated to operating under Dr. Deming's philosophy of management, including extensive application of statistical techniques and team-building efforts. We intend to be innovative and to allocate resources to fulfill the long-range needs of the customer and the company. We will institute better job training, including the help of statistical methods and will 'do it right the first time' eliminating scrap and waste. We will provide a vigorous program for retraining people in new skills, to keep up with changes in materials, methods, design of products, and machinery, and in the use of statistical techniques to identify areas of improvement. We will reduce fear by encouraging open two-way communication. We renounce the old philosophy of accepting defective workmanship in everything we do — paperwork, processes, and hardware. We must eliminate the dependence on mass inspection for quality. We will maximize the use of statistical knowledge and talent in both our division and our suppliers. We will demand and expect suppliers to use statistical process control to ensure quality. Where possible, we will single-source purchased items with the supplier who demonstrates the highest level of quality through statistical means."

As an observer of the human condition, I was struck by the statement renouncing old, ineffective habits. As a statistician, I was struck by the use of the word "statistical" six times in the statement of principles to which an engineering company has "committed and dedicated" itself. Before General Manager Bill Hoglund found Dr. Deming, statistical methods and statistical thinking were perhaps the last resources anyone at Pontiac considered for increasing productivity and competitive posture.

CHAPTER 3

**STATISTICAL METHODS FOR TAPPING INTO
THE INFORMATION FLOW GENERATED
BY A PROCESS**

"When you can measure what you are speaking about and express it in numbers, you know something about it; but when you cannot measure it, when you cannot express it in numbers, your knowledge is of a meagre and unsatisfactory kind."

Lord Kelvin; May 3, 1883

Statistics is the essence of the scientific method and relates to almost everything we do. It is a discipline that deals with chance and choice, with trade-offs, with cause and effect, and with predicting future events from a collection of facts and numbers.

Statistics was used, as told in the Bible, when Joseph devised a plan for allocation to the Egyptian people of grain collected in "good years," but it was not until the 1920s that statistics began to develop as an organized discipline. This development came about in large part through the efforts of a Cambridge-educated English scholar, Ronald Aylmer Fisher, whose work in designing agricultural experiments and in the application of the theory of genetics led him to develop a theoretical framework for prediction by statistical methods. His thinking struck so many as electrifying, that eventually people came from all over the world to study with him at the University of London.

Among those who traveled to London to learn from Fisher,

who was later knighted, was W. Edwards Deming; he had been exposed to a smattering of statistical methodology during his training in engineering, thermodynamics and astronomy. What Dr. Deming gleaned from Fisher's lectures, together with many later experiences and his fascination with the theory of statistical process control, led to the development of the statistical core of the Deming philosophy. This statistical core has defined a way of life in Japanese industry.

On a visit to the Tokai Rika Company in Japan a few years ago, Dr. Deming learned that the personnel there were using well over 200 control charts and that these charts were being reviewed every two months to see if they were doing what was needed, i.e., highlighting local problems so that manufacturing processes could be brought under control and then continually improved. He told me not long ago that control charts are being used in Japan more and more as time goes by.

Our experiences in November, 1982, in visiting the Deming prize winners, certainly were in keeping with these observations. During the Yokogawa Hewlett Packard plant tour, among the first things we were shown were some computer-generated control charts. Space dividers throughout the YHP facility were covered by so many multi-colored statistical charts that an almost festive appearance was created. And at the Kajima Corporation headquarters, the film about company-wide quality control was liberally sprinkled with shots of people using statistical techniques to help them identify problems and to improve their processes.

In 1980, an interviewer from *Quality* magazine asked Dr. Deming how well statistical techniques are being applied in this country. His response was not encouraging.

"I have no way of coming to any figure, but I will say that there is little understanding in this country of what quality control really is.

"Take the computer for example — it's both a curse and a blessing. It's a curse because it has led management to believe that, because they know from computer sheets that yesterday a particular production line made ten percent defectives, they have quality control. Nothing could be further from the truth. I can tell you about one plant where each morning the plant manager had on his desk a report of the number of defective items that his plant made the day before. The report might have said the average measurement was thus and so, the standard deviation was 13.1, the fourth moment standardized was 7.8. This information was of no use whatsoever to the poor man.

"The plant manager has the devil's own job — he has everything to look after. Besides production, there might be a man from the EPA who says that the plant put out too much smoke yesterday. Or there might be someone from OSHA waiting to see him because there was a complaint of an unsanitary condition. He has everything in the world to look after, and here's another one dumped in his lap.

"Very properly, after a little while, he disregards the computer printout. Now the same piece of electronic machinery and another $50,000 or $150,000 worth of brains — whatever it might take — could get him a short report that would tell him that at ten o'clock yesterday morning something went wrong on the line. At the same time, a new supplier's material went into use; the reason for the problem is a characteristic of the new material.''

Later the interviewer said that a comment frequently heard is that we need fewer statistical techniques and more common sense. Dr. Deming had no difficulty squelching that idea.

"One of the chapters in my new book is entitled, 'The Hazards of Common Sense.' Common sense cannot be measured. You have to be able to define and measure what is significant. Without statistical methods you don't know what the numbers mean.''

A similar point was made by William Conway, the former Chief Executive Officer of the Nashua Corporation, in 1980 during a panel discussion on Productivity. He pointed out that one of the greatest handicaps of people who are trying to improve productivity and quality is that they attempt to deal with these matters in generalities. The use of statistics is a way of getting into specifics that will allow managers and workers to make decisions based on facts rather than "speculation and hunches." He told his audience that statistics provide a road map to assist in solving problems and direct attention of managers to what is wrong with their processes.

"Unaided by statistical techniques, management's normal reaction to trouble is to blame the worker. This gives rise to the myth that there would be no problems in production or service if only workers would do their jobs correctly. In the vast majority of cases, individual workers are powerless to act because they are faced with problems that are built into the system of operation."

Conway made some of these same observations to me when I visited the Nashua Corporation in late 1982 to observe firsthand how the Deming philosophy was being put into operation there. At Nashua, Lloyd Nelson, the founding editor of the *Journal of Quality Technology,* told me about the working of the corporation's Quality Program that he spearheads. Dr. Deming had recommended Nelson to Conway for this endeavor after the latter was inspired by Deming and his philosophy.

In what Conway has called "a new way of managing the business," Nelson says that at quarterly operations reviews, charts of various kinds, including statistical control charts, are expected. No longer, he says, is a reporting manager able to get away with an essentially meaningless statement like, "This quarter we had quite a few problems that gave us a down-scale effect on our profit picture; but we think we've got our arms around the difficulties and look forward to an improved next quarter."

Training in statistical methods at Nashua began with the advent of the Quality Program. The policy currently specifies more than 10 hours of training in statistical techniques, on company time, for every one of their employees working in or near the company headquarters in Nashua, New Hampshire.

The statistical education program includes instruction in process-control methods, as well as in simpler techniques for identifying and solving problems. As the Nashua employees have become more sophisticated in statistical thinking, courses in more advanced subjects like "design of experiments" have been added. Knowing how to design experiments helps investigators avoid the problem of collecting data from which they can make little sense and allows them to get the most out of their research dollars. Agriculture, for instance, is one of the few industries in the U.S. that uses statistical design of experiments extensively. Interestingly enough, the U.S. has dominated and continues to dominate the world in agricultural production. Proficiency in the statistical design and interpretation of experiments is a prerequisite for managerial advancement in Japan.

At Nashua's Computer Products Division with its many engineers "on the cutting edge of technology," as Nelson describes them, it has been relatively easy to install statistical methodology throughout the plant. And this division of Nashua had, in the recession of 1982, its most profitable year to that date. In other parts of the company, including the overseas divisions, there has been progress, though it has been less dramatic.

In one conversation that I had with Dr. Nelson, he talked about some of the non-statistical aspects of the Quality Program. He pointed out that it uses both good personnel techniques and good industrial engineering techniques: "The trick is not to use an industrial design or industrial engineering technique when something else is called for. Don't set a pace when you need to get the thing in control. And of course there are reverse examples as well. Don't try to get the process under control when it isn't worth anything to begin with."

Nelson's admonition relates to point #12 of the Deming philosophy, having to do with the barriers to pride of workmanship, like inherited defectives and lack of operational job descriptions. All such barriers need to be attacked and overcome before one should attempt to install statistical methods.

While at Nashua, I realized that William Conway and Lloyd Nelson, with Dr. Deming as a catalyst and injector of ideas, had truly revolutionized the way Nashua does business. And the Nashua employees are enjoying the experience. Nelson told me in early 1983, when the company was undergoing financial reorganization, that one of the chief concerns of the union representatives was that the Quality Program would be retained. It is little wonder that William Conway calls Dr. Deming "The founder of the third wave of the industrial revolution."

Clearly, having a statistician on staff is a necessary ingredient for company-wide transformation. The Nashua Corporation, however, was able to use statistical methods to make a rather dramatic improvement in productivity even before Nelson joined the company. This involved paper coating operations in their plant at Merrimack, New Hampshire, somewhat removed, both physically and operationally, from the newer Computer Products Division that Lloyd Nelson described. Dr. Deming had recommended Charles A. (Charlie) Bicking, a consultant in Quality Control to help with the resolution of the problem of maintaining uniformity of coating material applied to carbonless paper.

Lloyd Nelson told me that Nashua began making waxed paper in the thirties, and coating things is still one of their major areas of expertise. When Charlie Bicking and I talked about his experiences at Nashua, he said, "The fellow who coats paper there may also coat aluminum. They will coat with almost anything that will stick on anything else."

In a speech delivered in Rio de Janeiro in March, 1981, William Conway described the paper coating problem and its solution. Water based coating containing various chemicals is applied to a moving web of paper. If the amount of coating is right, a good consistent mark can be made on the paper. The coating head applied approximately three pounds of dry coating to 3000 square feet of paper at a speed of approximately 1400 linear feet per minute on a web six or eight feet wide.

Technicians took samples of paper and made tests to determine the intensity of the mark. These tests were made on the sample, both as it came off the coater and after it was aged in an oven to simulate use by the customer. When tests showed the intensity of the mark to be too low or too high, the operator made adjustments that would increase or decrease the amount of coating material. Frequent, costly stops for new settings were a way of life.

The engineers knew that the average weight of the coating material was too high. Because of large variability in the process, however, they didn't know how to lower it without the risk of applying insufficient coating. A new coating head, to cost $700,000, was under consideration. There would be, besides the cost of $700,000, the time lost for installation and the risk that the new head might not achieve uniformity of coating any better than the equipment in use.

Finally, a decision to use statistical methods brought Charlie Bicking and Dr. Deming together to Merrimack. Charlie, having done statistical consulting for various paper companies over the years, was thoroughly familiar with paper coating. He told me why the undertaking had been so successful.

> "Number one, Charlie Clough, Nashua Group Vice President sat in on all of the meetings, so we got together a crack team. There were the manager of the plant, the production manager and some of the chemists and engineers. We would sit around a long table and talk about how we were going to put a control chart on the production process. The first thing we had to do was to get some data so that we could set control limits and lay down the flat rule that nobody would adjust the process unless it went outside the control-chart limits.

"Charlie Clough said, 'We're going to stop trying to control this process by waiting until we get the product sent into the lab and making a mark. We're going to control this by weight.' And that's what we did."

Charlie Bicking pointed out that sampling from this process was different from sampling piece parts like screws or washers. During the course of an eight-hour shift, four or five jumbo rolls are coated. Each one weighs, perhaps, 3,000 pounds and ultimately is worth about $6,000. Samples were taken and weighed at the beginning and end of each roll as the process was allowed to operate without adjustment.

It was thereby found that the coating head, if left untouched, was actually in pretty good statistical control at the desired level of 3.0 dry pounds of coating on the paper, plus or minus 0.4 pounds. Before the introduction of statistical control methods, the operator of the coating head had been over-adjusting his machine, putting on more coating, or less, in accordance with the results of the laboratory tests. In doing his best, following the instructions given to him, he was doubling the variation in the amount of coating. After statistical methods were introduced, elimination of various causes of extreme variation, highlighted by points outside the control limits, reduced the amount of coating required, and still good consistent quality was maintained. As a result of these actions, the coater distributed an average of 2.8 pounds per 3000 square feet, thereby saving 0.2 pounds on the average for every 3000 square feet, or $800,000 per year at then present volume and cost levels.

The story does not end here. Getting the process under statistical control opened the way for engineering improvements, and step by step, engineers and chemists modified the chemical content of the coating material so that less and less could be used. Without statistical control, the process was in unstable chaos, so there was almost no chance to detect the effects of improvement in the system. Once statistical control was achieved, it was easy to measure the effect of small changes in the chemistry of the coating and in the coating head. They thereby improved the coating head and achieved greater and greater uniformity of coating. All the while, statistical control of the coating was maintained at ever decreasing levels. All of this was accomplished without the purchase of a new head, i.e., without making the proposed capital investment of $700,000.

Today only 1.0 pound of improved coating is used, on the average, per 3,000 square feet of paper. This level is safe, as the variation lies only between 0.9 and 1.1. Since reduction of a tenth of a pound means an annual reduction of $400,000 in the cost of coating, the total savings is now $8,000,000 per year.

This massive lowering of expenditure is an impressive consequence of the use of statistical methods. However, Dr. Deming told me about an experience of his that produced an even more dramatic result for a company.

In late 1981, while he was working with a firm that makes electric motors, he learned that they were negotiating to buy machinery that would cost $25,000,000 and would provide better testing for a motor at a midway point in the manufacturing process. If a motor passes the point where the testing is done and is defective in any of about 50 ways, then the cost further along the assembly line, because of rework that will be needed, is about $500. He explained:

> "The people who were negotiating to purchase the $25,000,000 set-up were only trying to do their job — doing their best to avoid the cost of $500 further on in the

process. Now with a little figuring, including the interest on $25,000,000, you might say that this would be a good investment because the company was turning out 4000 motors a day for many different customers. The interest on the purchase price is about $10,000 per day, and that would include Saturdays, Sundays and holidays. The motors are probably turned out only 5 days a week. Still, you could be conservative and say that the interest would come to $2.50 for each of the 4000 motors produced.

"There would also be maintenance and depreciation on the apparatus, which would be far greater than the interest to pay. It seems, nevertheless, that it might be a bright idea to purchase it. Suppose that the cost was $6 or $7 per motor. You'd have manpower to pay for, and all told it would then cost about $50 to test the motor — maybe $40 without this new apparatus, $50 if you do have it. And with the present method of tests, defective motors do slip through, only a very few, but each one of them that's defective costs $500 to fix later on. It seems like a lot of money to spend, but the right thing to do.

"However, it is very clear that the statistician needs not reams of figures, not reams of machine sheets, but only one additional piece of information to make a decision. One needs to know the proportion of defective motors that come into this first point. And that was about one in 150. Now, that they knew, or they found the figure by studying the records. I'm talking about men that know their business. They know everything but how to do the job!"

From the figure of one defective motor per 150 on the average, one can easily calculate that the cost of not testing is

$500 divided by 150, or about $3.33, on the average, for each of the 4000 motors produced per day. Clearly, this is much less than the $50 cost for testing each of the 4000 motors. In fact, the savings by eliminating testing altogether is an average of about $46.67 per motor, or about $186,000 per day.

Dr. Deming discusses this in "Plan for Minimum Total Cost for Test Materials and Final Product," which makes up Chapter 13 of his 1982 book, "Quality, Productivity and Competitive Position." In this chapter, he speaks of the necessity in most practical cases of "all or none" sampling for minimizing costs, and he cites a paper of Alexander Mood published in the *Annals of Mathematical Statistics* in 1943. Mood refers to the average fraction defective, p, the cost to inspect one item, k1, and the cost of an escaping item in terms of dismantling, repairing, reassembling, etc., k2. In the above example, p = 1/150, k1 = $50 and k2 = $500. Mood's results imply that for a process in control, cost is minimized with no sampling when p is less than k1/k2 and minimized with 100% sampling when p is greater than k1/k2.

It seems fairly clear in this case that there was little chance that p, the average fraction defective, would increase from 1/150 to greater than 1/10, the value of k1/k2. Only if such were to happen should the management consider testing with the proposed new equipment.

After Dr. Deming gave his recommendation to stop testing to the company management, they cancelled the order for the new test equipment. In so doing, they saved $186,000 per day, plus interest, amortization and maintenance of $25 million worth of equipment!

"They told me a few days later they had broken off

all talks on such a thing; they were not going to buy it. But, they said, two of their competitors bought. Well, that's all right. It's a free country. People can do as they please. However, the cost of a mistake in free enterprise is that you get beat up.''

Sometime in the late summer of 1982, I read about another interesting instance of productivity improvement brought about by Deming intervention, in this case at the Genesco Corporation. At about the same time, Dr. Deming phoned to say that he would be going to Nashville to see the Genesco people, and asked if I would join the talks. Following a meeting at the offices of the Genesco subsidiary, Johnston and Murphy, with its president Bill Dragon and the managers of the various major departments, I learned some details of the parent company's initial success with the Deming methods.

These methods were first implemented, shortly after John L. Hannigan joined the company as Chairman in 1977, at a Genesco shoe-manufacturing plant in Pulaski, Tennessee. The program began with classes held in the evenings for all their plant management people.

After the managers learned something about statistics, they were ready for the second phase, the development of an 'operational description' for every operation in the plant. Then with the implementation of Phase Two, operators became aware of what was expected of them, and they began to think of quality product as an important and, above all, a realizable goal.

The third phase was to set up a statistical program in order to monitor and chart results of the critical operations in the plant, so that quality problems could be discovered before they created any new problems. To do this, the Pulaski plant now has four statistical inspectors who each day inspect certain shoes picked at random, checking the work in any operation which is critical to quality, or where problems are likely to occur. Each operator has one bundle or rack of work inspected at random four or five times per day.

Once a week, each department manager sits down with the assistant plant manager, who is primarily responsible for statistical quality control in the plant, and looks over the charts from his or her department. First, they look to see if any particular operation is showing defects above acceptable limits. It is expected that there will be variations from day to day, but if a consistently high number of defects shows up, they investigate to see what is causing the problem.

Next, the department manager looks for signals, for instance, an operator who systematically displays significantly more than the expected number of defects or a sudden increase in defects. If the manager notes a problem, he discusses it with the operator. Sometimes a machine may be out of adjustment or a particular pattern may be giving the operator trouble. Perhaps more training is needed.

One of the early problems discovered had to do with the ½ inch of leather required to extend over the last, the plastic mold around which the shoe is made. The department manager could tell by looking at the control chart that it was not a problem caused by an operator because all of them were having the same problem. It turned out that the pattern for the shoes was not large enough to include the required allowance. New patterns were made and the problem was solved.

As in the majority of the cases, the problem was the system, not the workers. Dr. Deming told me that quite a number of years ago he came upon a situation that was similar, both in that it involved a manufacturer of shoes and that the cause of the problem was the system.

In this case, the workers who were sewing together parts of shoes were causing difficulties because they continued to break thread in their sewing machines. Management was blaming the employees for incorrect adjustment of tension in the machines, but control charts revealed that the problem could not be traced to particular individuals or particular machines. It turned out that the purchasing agents had been instructed to buy on the basis of lowest price and that the culprit was the cheap thread supplied to all the workers and all the machines. Substitution of higher quality thread solved the problem and improved the quality of the shoes.

One might ask if the shoes being manufactured at Pulaski are really better now than they were before the quality-control program started. The employees there are convinced that they are. According to the packing room manager and the line quality auditor, they're sold on the program and they're proud of the shoes they're making.

All except one of the preceding cases dealt with increases in productivity resulting from the use of statistical control charts to identify causes of deficient quality. There are, however, other simpler techniques that can be used with data to help anyone understand a given process and to identify associated problems, assign priorities and find possible causes. One of the few books that describe these is "Guide to Quality Control" by Kaoru Ishikawa, the son of the 1950 president of Kei-dan-ren and the brother of the current president of the Kajima Corporation which we visited in 1982. William Conway also describes these methods in his "Call to Arms" talk that is available as part of

M.I.T.'s video-tape series on the Deming approach to quality, productivity and competitive position.

In Japanese companies that have won the Deming Prize, like the Kajima Corporation, Yokogawa Hewlett Packard and the Rhythm Watch Company, everyone in the firm from the very top to the bottom is familiar with these statistical tools and with the use of control charts. Some companies even issue little pocket-size booklets containing summaries of these methods.

Charlie Bicking and I talked about some of these techniques, which are taught at several of the U.S. companies that have embraced the Deming philosophy, for example Nashua, Pontiac and Ford, to provide an organized approach to solving problems. We discussed flow charts, Pareto diagrams, cause and effect diagrams, run charts, scattergrams and histograms, examples of some of which are shown on page 80. Charlie Bicking discussed flow charts first.

"The first question you've got to answer is, 'What is happening in the process?' You have to understand the underlying physical process and know what it does. To get a handle on this, you flow chart the process. It doesn't have to be a fancy diagram that an industrial engineer would draw with all the circles and squares and triangles and so forth. But you have to identify all the operations, the material flow loops, the information flow loops, where samples are taken, what measurements are taken, and all the details. For example, in the paper coating process, what do they do with those pieces when they go from one machine to another? Are they putting them back on and rerolling them, or turning them around? Flow-charting is helpful for any process you can think of."

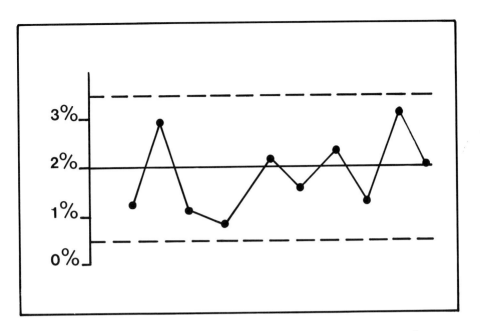

Fig. 1. Control chart for the percentage of loose connections.

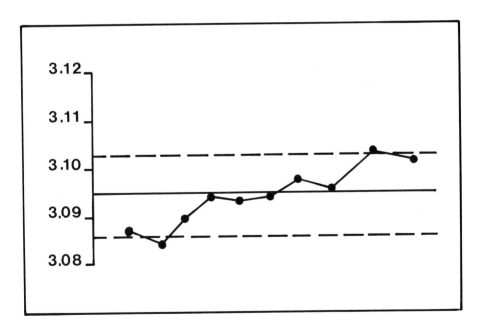

Fig. 2. Control chart for disc diameters.

73

At the Shionogi Pharmaceutical Co., 1955.

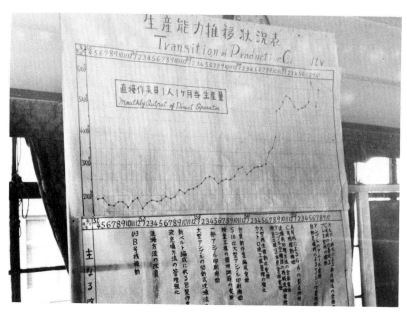

Chart showing increase in production per worker at the Takeda
Pharmaceutical Company in 1955.

With Mr. Kano, expert interpreter, at the eight-day course in Tokyo, 1950.

Deming lecture with standing room only, at the Nagoya Chamber of Commerce, 1951.

With officers of the Toyo Cotton Spinning Company, 1951.

With officers of the Tanabe Pharmaceutical Company, 1951.

First Deming Award ceremonies, at Osaka, September, 1951.

The eight-day course in Tokyo, 1950. Dr. Nishibori in the background.

A 1984 Deming seminar at the Ford Motor Company.

The most famous name in Japanese quality control is American.

His name is Dr. W. Edwards Deming, and he's a quality control expert.

In 1950, the Union of Japanese Scientists and Engineers (JUSE) invited Dr. Deming to lecture several times in Japan, events that turned out to be overwhelmingly successful.

To commemorate Dr. Deming's visit and to further Japan's development of quality control, JUSE shortly thereafter established the Deming Prizes, to be presented each year to the Japanese companies with the most outstanding achievements in quality control.

Today, Dr. Deming's name is well known within Japan's industrial community, and companies compete fiercely to win the prestigious Demings.

In 1953, Sumitomo Metals was fortunate enough to win the Deming Prize For Application. In retrospect, we believe it may have been the single most important event in the history of quality control at Sumitomo. By inspiring us to even greater efforts, it helped us to eventually become one of the world's largest and most advanced steel-makers.

Sumitomo Metals owes a great deal to the American quality control expert who became one of Japan's greatest inspirations. On that point, the management and employees of Sumitomo Metals would like to take this opportunity to say simply, "Thanks, Dr. Deming, for helping to start it all."

DEMING PRIZE COMMITTEE, JUSE

DEMING MEDAL

THE RIGHT QUALITY & UNIFORMITY ARE FOUNDATIONS OF COMMERCE, PROSPERITY & PEACE W. EDWARDS DEMING

◆ SUMITOMO METALS

SUMITOMO METAL INDUSTRIES, LTD. Tokyo & Osaka, Japan   Sumitomo Metal America, Inc. Head Office 420 Lexington Ave. New York, N.Y. 10017. U.S.A   Phone (212) 949-4760   Offices in Los Angeles, Chicago, Houston
MAIN PRODUCTS Tubes & pipe, flat rolled products, bars, shapes & wire rods, rolling stock parts, steel castings & forgings, and a wide range of steel products

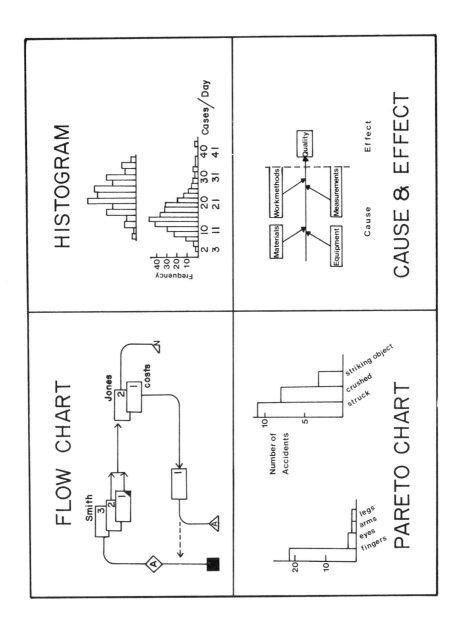

FLOW CHART

HISTOGRAM

PARETO CHART

CAUSE & EFFECT

Top left, Dr. Lloyd S. Nelson of the Nashua Corporation, discussing Pareto charts with representatives of Nashua de Mexico.

81

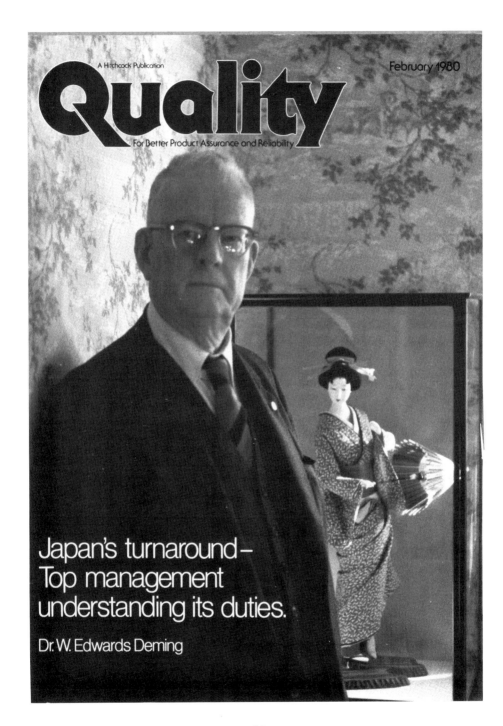

A Hitchcock Publication

February 1980

Quality

For Better Product Assurance and Reliability

Japan's turnaround– Top management understanding its duties.

Dr. W. Edwards Deming

On his 83rd birthday at the Pontiac Motor Division, G.M., with Ron Moen and General Manager Bill Hoglund.

NOVEMBER 1984 $2.00

W. EDWARDS DEMING
America's Sage
On Quality In
Production

84

Dr. Deming with the author, 1985.

85

INQUIRER

MARCH 11, 1984

The Philadelphia Inquirer Magazine

W. EDWARDS DEMING

WANTS TO MAKE
AMERICA
WORK AGAIN

BY MARY WALTON

HE DID IT FOR JAPAN.
WHY SHOULDN'T HE DO IT FOR US?

Clockwise from left: Bill Scherkenbach and President Don Petersen of the Ford Motor Company, Dr. Deming and Vice President Jim Bakken.

87

THE
W. EDWARDS DEMING
INSTITUTE OF
NEW ZEALAND

FOR
IMPROVEMENT OF
QUALITY AND PRODUCTIVITY
IN NEW ZEALAND MANUFACTURING
AND SERVICE INDUSTRIES

Brochure for New Zealand Deming Institute.

Badge for attendees of Deming roundtable discussion at U.S. Naval Air Rework Facility, 1985.

Charlie Bicking made the point that there is almost never anyone in an organization who can tell you accurately what the total process is and that in flow charting production processes, the production people sometimes get some startling surprises. He went on:

> "The second thing you want to know is what the big problems are. And I'll tell you, when you begin to talk to people about what the problems are, they don't discriminate well between the problems, the symptoms, and the causes. So it's important that some data be collected and put together in some kind of analysis that can help identify the problems and give you a priority rating for them. Making a Pareto diagram, which is a bar chart that enables someone readily to identify the few vital problems as contrasted to the many trivial ones, is a way of doing this."

An illustration of a typical Pareto analysis, with followup, was given by Hewlett Packard's C.E.O. John A. Young in his article in the August, 1985 issue of *Quality Progress*. It involved HP's computer support operation, which is responsible for supplying repair parts and exchange assemblies for all HP computers worldwide. Young reports that until 1984, because their response time wasn't fast enough, this operation had a less than enviable reputation with their customers, who are HP field sales engineers. Using a Pareto analysis, they found that 85% of their delay resulted from waiting for just 20% of the parts they needed.

Since the parts in question came from other HP divisions, the computer support operation took an educational road show around the company. It consisted of "mapping" the entire process of repairing customer orders — from customer, to HP sales engineer, to computer support operation and back to other HP divisions. In effect, they flow-charted the process in the manner Charlie Bicking described. This allowed the other divisions to appreciate the importance of their role in computer support and motivated them to see that the vital parts are now supplied on time. Thus, the important problems were identified and a means for improvement of the situation was found.

Charlie Bicking talked about a particular technique for finding the causes of problems:

"After you've identified an important problem, then you can ask, 'What are the causes of the problem?' A good graphical way to organize the thinking about the causes of the problem is the 'cause and effect diagram,' also called the 'fishbone diagram,' or the 'Ishikawa diagram.' This is a statistical technique that the Japanese invented.

"This diagram can provide organized methods for attacking problems that are more effective than simply brainstorming. Consider possible causes (bones attached to the backbone) of a problem (the head of the fish) in terms of materials, machines, measurements, methods and people, 4 m's and a p. It used to be 5 m's before the feminist movement.

"First you consider all the things about materials that might cause the problem that are costing money, then all the elements of the plant equipment that might be the cause. What about measurement? Believe me, measurements are very often the cause of major problems.

"Next, methods. Do they have written methods?

Often, they don't, or they're so old, that nobody looks at them anymore. Or there have been so many engineering change orders that nobody knows what the methods are. And then finally you consider the workers.''

In any Deming exchange with hourly workers, one can notice that the 4 m's and the p include most everything about which the workers complain. And as outlined later, these are among the elements that are of particular concern in allocating company resources to attain the long-term goals of the organization. In different situations, the potential causes of problems can, of course, be organized differently on an Ishikawa diagram. Charlie Bicking continued.

"You may want to ask, 'What's the process doing now? So you begin to plot, a control chart or simply a line plot. You can learn a lot just with a line plot, plotting the production-process data in some kind of sequence, chronological or by machine or lot, etc. You can see a lot of things that nobody ever knew were going on there. Maybe it's high every Monday and low every Friday. One of the things you see most frequently is the process making big shifts above the average for a period of time, and then below. You don't have an average on the chart yet, but you can see it's down here at one time and up at another.

"You begin to learn something about what's going on in the production process. The people in operations don't know. They've got some kind of engineering specification, which they very often can't meet. And all they're doing is beating their brains out, wearing their system out and adding variation to the process by constantly adjusting it. And this is true whether it is manual adjustment or controlled by some kind of instrumental readout or feedback. Most of these feedback and control machines are terrible. A lot of them are not turned on most of the time because the operator doesn't trust them. They're good machines usually, but they're not maintained. There's nobody around the plant anymore that knows how they work because the guy that used to do this has gone off somewhere else.''

We talked next about scattergrams, the simple two-dimensional point plots that show the statistical relationship between two variables, moisture content and elongation of thread, for example. We did not discuss some of the more sophisticated techniques that can be used for exploiting the potential information pool in a process, like "cumulative sum" charts for identifying shifts, weighted and unweighted running averages and other means of detecting trends, or EVOP (evolutionary operation) involving small changes in a process persisting long enough so that responses can be well measured. Before our conversation ended, though, we discussed a technique for getting a look at what's happened in a process recently, a "histogram," which Charlie Bicking described as a snapshot of the process. "A line plot can be a moving picture of what's going on," he said, "but this is going to be a snapshot."

He told me how the use of a histogram helped to show management the way the workers were attacking a particular tolerance problem in the absence of statistical control. A histogram, incidentally, shows values of a measured variable along the horizontal axis. Vertical bars demonstrate the relative frequency of occurrence for evenly spaced ranges of the variable. (See example on page 80.) In this case the variable was a critical dimension of a machine part measured in inches.

"There was an upper specification of 1.525 inches for a machine part and a lower specification, too. Actually, the part was the base plate for a disc drive, and the specification applied to a dimension that was critical because they were going to match the head mechanism and the drive mechanism for the disc. And this was giving them terrible problems.

"We drew a histogram of the measured values of this dimension, and there was a perfect left half of a bell-shaped curve smack up against this upper tolerance of 1.525 inches. I said, 'Where did the rest of it go?' Then the rest of the data, down the scale around 1.522 inches formed another distribution, perfectly bell-shaped and symmetric. So there was a group of production people and engineers sitting around the room when I put this up on the blackboard. They had been having fits trying to match the parts. They were getting head crashes and all this kind of thing.

"After they had had a good look at the histogram, one of them said, 'Do you know what we do? We rework everything that's over 1.525 inches, and that perfect bell shaped symmetric distribution is a rework. That's the answer.'"

The problem was that they were making this part too large on the first try. They preferred to make it thick rather than make it right, because then it could be reworked. If it happened to be too small, they couldn't rework it and they'd have to scrap it. So they were reworking everything that was over 1.525 inches, and doing a beautiful machine job on the rework. "Why couldn't they do it right the first time, that is, reduce the average diameter so as to avoid large amounts of rework?" Charlie

Bicking asked. "They could, but nobody had ever looked at it that way."

Looking at a process-behavior problem in a way that allows one to extract the important information generated by the process is an integral part of statistical process control. For a study at Rockwell International's Science Center, made for an Arizona power company, this philosophy was the guiding principle. Solution of the problem in this case depended upon a histogram's helping to unlock the mystery of why a process seemed to be behaving in an unexpected way.

The project had to do with the prediction of levels of concentration of sulfur in the air resulting from burning coal in an enormous electric power plant in the middle of the Arizona desert. An environmental organization was suing the public utility company that owned the power plant because it felt the urban standards of air quality, which had been prescribed for this empty desert area, were not being met. These standards seemed very stringent at the time, but in light of what has been learned recently about acid rain, they were probably justified.

The power plant had cost about a billion dollars to build, and if the environmental organization won the suit, the power company would have to spend an additional $200 million for "scrubbers" to wash sulfur out of the coal before it was burned. If this was to be done, then a different environmental problem would result in the formation of pools of sulfuric acid that would require disposal costing additional millions of dollars; the exact amount could not be determined.

Because of the vast amount of money at stake, dozens of high-level technical and managerial personnel at the public utility were dedicated to getting at the truth of the matter, hoping of course that this would result in a saving of the additional expense. Statisticians and chemists from the Environmental Protection Agency were assiduously monitoring the results.

As part of the study, airplanes were used to investigate the behavior of the plume formed by the burning coal. A consulting firm, knowledgeable in analysis of air circulation, was hired to determine the highest concentration of sulfur that one might observe in any spot on the desert nearby in a 3-year period. Important information in making this prediction was the concentration of sulfur in the coal in a nearby coal field which was to be mined and subsequently burned in the power plant. On the basis of preliminary measurements, the scrubbers seemed to be needed.

Sulfur concentrations were measured in 3 places in 3 different ways. First, core samples were taken in the coal fields by forcing shafts deep into the earth and bringing up coal from the different strata. The coal from each stratum was ground up and mixed well, and then a small sample from the mixture was put into a test tube and a determination of the level of sulfur concentration was made by weight. These determinations were then averaged for different areas within specified fields.

After coal was mined, it was given a coarse grinding, usually mixed with other coal from a nearby area or areas and shipped by train the 100 or so miles to the power plant. There the coal was ground up, again mixed and ground another time and mixed again before being subjected to daily sampling and sulfur analysis. The mixing and sampling procedures were designed in accordance with specifications of the ASTM (American Society for Testing and Materials). Finally, the concentration of sulfur in the air resulting from burning coal at the power plant was also measured.

Results were available from analyses of core samples and corresponding daily averages of coal at the plant for 3 different large mines that had provided coal in the recent past. The numbers of values of both core-sample averages and power-plant daily averages were all quite large; and calculations showed that for each of the 3 pairs of these large samples from the 3 different mining areas, the average sulfur concentration for the core samples was significantly larger than the corresponding average for the power-plant coal. These differences had been ignored by power company personnel because there seemed to be no apparent explanation for the phenomenon.

The largest sample consisted of 1700 daily observations, enough to get a good picture of the frequency distribution of the sulfur concentration by making a histogram showing the number of occurrences for ranges of levels of sulfur content. The distribution was narrow and looked almost like a bell-shaped curve, but was not quite symmetric and had thin trailing tails on either end. The distributions for the core samples looked similar, but they were considerably more spread out.

If the sample had been quite small, one would probably, in analyzing it, have made the assumption that the distribution was Gaussian. But, because of the large number of observations available, the lack of symmetry and the trailing tails were evident from the histograms.

Identification of the type of distribution from which the data were selected seemed a possible means of helping to explain the discrepancies in the averages of the mine and power-plant sulfur concentrations. But the distribution had only one really distinctive property, the thin, trailing tails.

During a conversation with Ray Schafer, one of the co-authors of the book, "Methods for Statistical Analysis of Reliability and Life Data," the coal study and this particular aspect of the sulfur concentration samples were mentioned. He then said that the "inverted gamma" is a distribution with tails that are thin and trailing. Dr. Schafer had written about this distribution in a section of the book, where as elsewhere it is used in a theoretical context for making mathematical manipulations. Methods described in the book were used to fit all 6 sample data sets of sulfur concentration to the inverted gamma distribution; and the fit turned out to be incredibly good.

To estimate the mean of an inverted gamma distribution, one uses the harmonic, rather than the arithmetic mean of the data. Thus, one inverts each observed value, calculates the average (the arithmetic mean) then inverts the result. The harmonic mean is always less than the arithmetic mean, and the more spread out the distribution, the greater the discrepancy between the two kinds of sample means.

For each of the 3 available sample data sets, the harmonic means of the core samples and of the power-plant samples were nearly equal, and, of course, less than the arithmetic means of the core-sample values. For the power-plant coal, the harmonic mean in each of the 3 cases was only slightly less than the corresponding arithmetic mean, reflecting the small amount of dispersion in the distribution due to all the mixing that had taken place.

Why was the harmonic mean of the core samples the correct average to use and why did it predict so well the sulfur concentrations in the plant coal? The answer lay in an incorrect tacit assumption that was made in averaging determinations by weight of sulfur in coal. In doing this averaging, one presumes that the densities of both the coal and the sulfur, i.e., the weights per given volume, are constant.

The assumption is valid for the sulfur, but not for the coal. Actually, a large number of people who worked for the power company and who were involved in this study knew that in the fields the coal was made up of a combination of organic and inorganic substances, with very different densities. In fact, density of the coal was one of the many variables that was measured for every sample.

It turned out that volume (or weight) of the sulfur per volume of coal (vc) was fairly fixed, so that the random variation in the measurements of the weight of sulfur (ws) per weight of coal (wc) was primarily a result of the variation in the coal density (wc/vc). Since ws/wc = (ws/vc)/(wc/vc), the variation in ws/wc, the random variable actually measured, is accounted for in the denominator on the right side of the equation — the coal density. This explains why the harmonic means of the mine sulfur concentrations, so much lower than their arithmetic means, predicted the power-plant coal averages so well.

The result of the study made the critical difference. The amount of sulfur in the coal was shown to be less than originally calculated, so that the $200 million investment in the scrubbers by the power company was found to be unnecessary. Besides this, any environmental problems that might have been caused by such an installation were thus non-existent, and presumably, the subscribers were also spared an increase in rates.

CHAPTER 4

**PEOPLE, MACHINES, METHODS
AND MATERIALS**

". . . when people who work can see the benefit of what they do, and when they can enjoy the feeling of themselves in the doing of it well, and when they can make the composition, they will say the work is good. But when they have none of these things the work is bad and it doesn't matter what it pays. It can pay in the six figures and you will sit there suspended in your misery, with your head in your hands."

E.L. Doctorow in *United* magazine, July, 1982.

In a 1981 interview that appeared in *Military Science and Technology,* Dr. Deming was asked whether Japanese management has advantages other than statistical quality systems and company loyalty. He answered that the Japanese worker knows what his job is and that probably 80 percent of American workers don't know and are afraid to ask.

"And why is the American worker afraid? Well, somebody trained him, maybe the foreman. But he still doesn't understand what to do. Or there is some material that is unsuited to the purpose. He asks for help two or three times, but the foreman never has any time or tells him, 'Well, it's the way I told you.' So the worker doesn't wish to be a trouble maker. He works in fear."

Dr. Deming minces no words when he speaks of supervisors who exhort employees to do their best. "Think of the chaos there would be, with everybody doing his best and not knowing what to do!''

Traditionally, the responsibility of the foreman in this country has been to keep up the production pace. But in the Deming philosophy, the foreman's job is to provide direction to the production workers and to report problems the workers may have, such as machines that are not maintained, inherited defects, poor tools, fuzzy operational definitions and the like. To accomplish this leadership role may require the use of control charts for pinpointing problems to which the workers may be oblivious. Rather than acting as expediters who put the fear of God into the people they supervise, foremen in this new role act as facilitators to help the workers build in quality and thereby increase productivity. They help the workers feel a sense of pride and pleasure in their work.

This may all sound a bit corny and idealistic, but in the companies where the hourly workers have experienced this kind of revolution, the change in attitude is remarkable to behold. As they have seen management taking care of problems that they've pointed out to their foremen and other supervisors, hourly workers have begun to realize that it's worth their while to strive for quality. One of Pontiac's plant supervisors, Clayton Williams, told me that ever since management had encouraged him to adopt the Deming philosophy so that the entire working procedure was changed in accordance with Dr. Deming's ideas, the changes have been as total as they have been beneficial.

There is now a common goal, understood and subscribed to by everyone in the company; and that is that each one has the right to be proud of his work, be it a gasket, be it an assembled engine, or be it a financial report. And with that, former barriers to productivity have come tumbling down. Nobody is worried anymore about turning out as much product as possible per shift, counting the pieces and hours. Each individual is seeing to it that every item is as good as it can possibly be, rework is hardly ever necessary, a product is well made when it is made, productivity is rising, the workers are proud of what they have accomplished, the customer has considerably fewer complaints and competitive position is enhanced. The people who formerly inspected items after they were finished, are now co-operating with all others to insure quality products. They are no longer acting as professional watchdogs to detect defects; they are now helping to prevent them. Control charts help everyone focus on the common goal, and co-operation and striving for quality and excellence have replaced rivalry, fear and shoddy workmanship.

In the spring of 1982 in Washington, during one of our discussions, Dr. Deming spoke of the phenomenon of fear — the fear of asking, of telling, of suggesting, of taking positive action. He told me about a seminar in which there were two women who had changed jobs. He thought that they probably didn't know each other before they changed, and maybe not until they came to the seminar. They changed jobs, the women told him, because they feared that any word they said or any question they asked that would appear to throw any doubt whatever on management would reflect on them in time. Perhaps not now, but there would be a time in the future when somebody would remember, and they would come out losers on some competition, a pay increase, a new job, or something of the sort. Whether it was true or not had nothing to do with the case, he felt. The women thought it was true. "They were in fear." In other words, they did not care to work for this company, and this company lost the benefits of their knowledge and experience. The women went to another firm which thus reaped the benefits of the knowledge and experience of these two.

I asked him about "driving out fear" as one of his 14 points. I wanted to know if it was included from the early days or noted more recently. He told me that it was William J. Latzko, Vice President of the Irving Trust Company, who, 4 or 5 years earlier had called his attention to the category of fear — that it was a category all by itself and deserved special mention. Dr. Deming read me a letter from the top of a pile of mail on his desk which pointed out that in less autocratic companies there is probably less fear, but in its place, there is something that can be equally devastating to quality and productivity — an attitude of indifference on the part of supervision and management. In such companies, the author of the letter observed, a worker will fail to report problems because the foreman and superintendent don't appear to be interested. They seem to care only about keeping up production.

People on an assembly line know that turning out junk by the numbers is not the right thing to do. They tend to know, on some level of consciousness, that such a policy will lose customers for the company and in the end will jeopardize their jobs. But in the face of continuing indifference to their problems on the part of management, workers will usually accept "production at any cost." It is this situation that is the principle cause of our perception of the American worker as one who is indifferent to the quality of the product turned out.

Yet, *Time,* March 30, 1981, reported on the success of the San Diego based Sony plant in producing quality products with American workers. The plant manager, Shiro Yamada, told a *Time* reporter that American workers are as quality conscious as the Japanese. And *Britannica Films* has made a documentary called "Participative Management" that shows how Japanese management in the Nissan pick-up truck plant in Smyrna, Tennessee attains levels of quality and productivity with American workers that U.S. bosses have not been able to achieve.

U.S. News and World Report, July 4, 1983, quoted a former Detroit assembly line worker, now employed at that Nissan plant, about his years in Detroit. "It was dog eat dog. You never knew when a supervisor was going to blame you for something he did, or when another employee would point the finger at you. It never stopped." At Nissan, he says, conditions are very different. "They don't play those games. They give you all the time in the world to do your job. If you can't do the job here, it's not the company's fault."

Such stories are being repeated over and over. By February 2, 1984, *USA Today* reported that 476 Japanese-owned companies employed almost 83,000 American workers. Often, the Japanese companies take over U.S. firms that find it impossible to remain profitable. For example, the *San Diego Mercury News,* November 9, 1983, quoted William Serrin's story in the *New York Times* about a television manufacturing plant that, in a plan to beat the competition, made what turned out to be an unsuccessful move from the Midwest to the Sun Belt. After a few years, the plant was sold to Sanyo, a Japanese company. Sanyo kept the same work force which, now in a managerial climate that promotes teamwork, turns out excellent TV sets at a high level of productivity. A veteran 12-year worker says, "We are a family."

Brian Joiner, in *Quality Progress,* May 1986, stresses the criticality of the feeling that everyone is working toward common goals. With such a feeling, he says, teamwork becomes pervasive.

During a meeting of top executives of a large manufacturing firm, I heard Dr. Deming address the topic of the attitude of workers towards quality production in American industry. He said that in contrast to what is generally believed, hourly workers feel that they are the only ones in their companies who are interested in quality. Only a few weeks later, W. Paul Tippett, Chief Executive Officer of American Motors, commented on one of PBS' MacNeil-Lehrer reports that Detroit automakers, who were then trying to convince their employees that quality is a number one priority, were learning that workers on auto assembly lines have felt for years that all management wanted was productivity at any cost.

At one time I might have felt that the Deming statement concerning management's indifference to quality was a bit of hyperbole and that the C.E.O. of American Motors was excessively negative in expressing similar sentiments concerning attitudes of the past. But then I listened to discussions of people at various levels of management and labor in U.S. industry. On several occasions, I heard the words of hourly workers interacting with Dr. Deming, and I became convinced that these views were not overly negative concepts of reality. I now believe that for the most part, management in American industry has succeeded over the years in communicating to their employees that quantity of product produced (whether it be a service or a commodity) is the only measure they consider important.

Not so long ago I taped a meeting of Dr. Deming with a very large group of hourly workers, and I have since witnessed several such meetings. On the basis of my own observations and the more extensive experience of Dr. Deming, I have concluded that the responses of the workers throughout the country, in no matter what industry or company, are almost always the same. They are all telling us essentially the same things. And underlying these messages is the fact that management has wanted quantity, not quality.

Dr. Deming's ingenuous manner and the fact that he obviously empathizes with his audience does not escape the attention of the attendees at these events. During the meeting from which the following collection of questions and answers came, I watched the general attitude of the audience change from something short of surliness and covert hostility to receptivity and something approaching joviality. There is no doubt that the workers, after a short indoctrination period, felt as comfortable with him as with their favorite uncle.

The individuals involved in this exchange, men for the most part, work in a very large U.S. company and, at the time of the taping, had been attending a "quality-of-working life" program for seven years. They had also participated for over a year in a "quality-circle" program designed to help them work together to solve problems and to communicate ideas to management for improving productivity. This is a company that had been making efforts for a long time to involve its hourly personnel in the company's problems. As we shall see, however, the hourly personnel did not perceive that management really cared about their feelings. The dialogue has been edited a bit to avoid repetitiousness.

Dr. Deming began this particular meeting with a question that was calculated to be not specific at all.

W.E. Deming: Does your industry face any problems? What are they?

Hourly Worker: Not selling enough of our products.

WED: Why do you suppose this is?

HW: Too much government control. Communication not good.

WED: Communication not good? What kind of communication are you looking for? Certainly you know what your job is.

HW: We know what our job is.

WED: Oh, you do! You're exceptional. If you know what your job is, what the heck's the trouble?

HW: The quality isn't what it should be.

WED: That's always true of course. Well, what is it that makes a difference?

HW: Workmanship.

WED: Well, you don't care. I mean, the customer bought the thing, so you have his money.

HW: We don't have as many customers as we used to have. We don't have the same customers.

WED: Well, as long as you get customers, it doesn't make any difference.

HW: We'd like to have the same ones back again.

WED: Repeat customers, ah ha!

HW: The costs of our products are too high.

WED: Why don't you just cut the price?

HW: The company has to make a profit.

WED: Well now, let's try to put some of these things together. The quality is not what the customer expects. Waste is in the system that produced it. Is that right? The price is too high for what the customer gets. Am I reading you right?

HW: Yes, not getting good value for the dollar.

WED: Well, what is there to do about it? Let me ask you another question. Is there such a thing as productivity? People talk about productivity all the time.

HW: What do you mean by productivity?

WED: Good question. How, as you improve quality do you improve productivity? Let me give it to you in two words: "Less rework." As you improve the quality you have less rework and less waste so the customer gets more for his money. My friend, Dr. Feigenbaum, a consultant in quality made a little study. It showed that the cost of most American products include from 10 to 40 percent waste. What does that do? It can slowly put American products out of business.

Last March on the day after St. Patrick's Day, I was at a Chamber of Commerce luncheon. There was a man sitting two places down from me, and I asked him what he did. He said he makes beer. "Well, that's good," I said. I mean that helps a lot of people. I asked him if he had any problems. "No, no problems." Well, he's the first man I've met, in I don't know how long, who had no problems.

I said, "That's most extraordinary! No color problems or cans cut wrong so that they jam the machine?" "No, we just set off the lot of defective cans that we can't use. Then the vendor comes and hauls them away and replaces them with good cans at his expense."

Isn't that great? At his expense. It never occurred to him that he and his customers were paying. The customer always pays for waste. Rework raises the cost. Somebody has to pay for it. So the job is to cut down on rework and get more productivity. You get that by raising quality. How do you do it? What is quality? Is it always clear what is acceptable?

HW: What's acceptable one day isn't always acceptable the next.

WED: "Right yesterday, wrong today." That's disconcerting, I know. What are needed are what I call "operational definitions" so that people can understand what is acceptable and what is not. And so that it will be the same tomorrow as today. Absolutely vital! Now what else is pretty vital?

HW: You should be able to do that job with the same feeling that you would do it at home. Like if you apply a part or do something, you want to be able to have the same pride on the job as you do at home.

WED: You sure do. Now, how can management help you to do a better job? Granted that you know what is acceptable quality and what is not.

HW: Training. Proper tools.

WED: I should think so. What else?

HW: Spare parts for whatever you're fixing. Get management to listen to the machine operator. Most of the time when you tell them something is wrong, they won't listen to you. You ask them to redo a machine or change a little bit on it to make it easier for your job. They won't listen to you. "That's just the way it is. We don't have the money. It costs too much." Give the operator a part to start with that's good.

WED: Give him stuff that's already defective, what can he do with it? It will be defective when he gets through with it. Sometimes, I know, you can fold material this way or that so as to hide a defect. But that takes time. The stuff has to be right before you start to work on it.

I know that some companies have slogans posted around, "Your work is your self-portrait. Would you sign it?" No, I wouldn't. Not I. Not with defective canvas to start with, paint not suited to the job and brushes that are worn out. I'm not going to sign it. No matter what I do it will still be defective. How could it be otherwise? It was defective before I got it.

Defects beget defects. Raw material has to come in right. Whatever you work on is raw material to you. What you send out, you send out to a customer. The next operator is your customer. If he gets something defective, what can he do with it? He can't take any pride in his work no matter what he does.

I know that this is absolutely fundamental. And you have to have tools. And somebody has to pay attention when the machine is out of order and do something about it. What else? What else can help people to do a better job?

HW: Have a commitment to excellence instead of a commitment to a policy.

WED: Yeah, but the policy is excellence.

HW: I don't think so.

WED: How can commitment to excellence help you when the stuff was defective when you got it, when your machine is out of order, when you're cramped and you don't have space to do your work and you don't have time to do it right? Commitment to excellence. You might as well throw it right out the window.

HW: Don't you feel the American public has been led to accept waste and deficiencies because we've never had the challenge before to do a better job?

The American public has never had to worry about waste and all that. Now they have to because of the competition. Your restaurants, you get twice as much as you need to eat. You don't buy recapped tires; you buy new tires. And that's all waste.

WED: Yes, that's all waste. But isn't there worse waste than that? More effective in ruining the standard of living in this country? And that is rework. Rework, which raises the price.

The tools have to be right in the first place. They have to stay right. Through your operation and on to the next and the next. Handling damage. Look at the accidents. He who thinks there will never be any accidents doesn't belong in this world. But what you're saying is that it's got to be right to start with and kept right; which means you gotta have the right tools, right machine, and you must know what the job is. Start right and keep it right. Sounds simple. Just try to do it. Can you think of any aids to help you?

HW: Training. Morale. They should have as much concern for us as they have for the machines we're operating. Morale in the last ten years has gotten lost in the production goals. Where you built 11,000 last year, it's 11,500 this year. They really don't care about us or the quality of the product.

WED: Don't care about the quality. Make 100 per day, no matter what. Does that damage morale? Well, it sure does in my judgment. I've talked to lots of people. I get around. And it sure does. One hundred, no matter what. Just get rid of it. Sell it. Anything you can get for it is all right. A work standard. You've heard of it. You know all about it? Can you name one? How many parts per hour?

HW: Three hundred parts per hour. Not good parts, just parts.

WED: What if you make 302? Then what?

HW: You get a longer break.

WED: Well do you have time off on this?

HW: Some lines are run so that when you get your production schedule, you take a break.

WED: Take a break? Play cards?

HW: Sure.

WED: Finish two hours before the whistle blows.

HW: It's conceivable. Yes.

113

WED: And you play cards. Meanwhile what do you think of the management?

HW: They're easy.

WED: You know that's building waste into the product. The machines are there. The company's paying interest on them, and they're idle. I've talked to people working under these conditions, and they don't like it. They know it's bad management. Isn't there anything you've heard of that will help people do a better job?

HW: Better communications between shifts and in general.

WED: That doesn't always solve problems, though. You may know by communicating that there's a problem, but that doesn't always throw any light on how to remove it. Aren't there any aids to help people on the job?

HW: Control methods on the process.

WED: Aha! A simple chart that will show anybody how he's doing. Whether he should make adjustments or, for heaven's sake, leave it alone. Isn't that what you meant? Once the basic difficulties are removed, the control chart will help you do a better job.

HW: People are always saying that it's the other guy's fault when there's a problem.

WED: Well, the control chart will help you with this. It will also tell you when to leave the system alone and when whatever fault there is belongs to the system. Suggestions on what to do. Or, you can see yourself when you were in error. And you can correct it. It enables a man to be the master of his work. Handicaps have to be removed first though before a control chart can make you master of your work. A control chart cannot help the person whose job it is to make defectives.

HW: What do you think about quality circles? Can you say something about them?

WED: Did quality circles report that the stuff they get to work on is already defective? They don't need to make more defectives. They've already got some. Some circles reported that? What else was it? Training, not enough space? Yes, I think quality circles in the presence of quality control can be very effective when the workers can see that management is trying to do its job.

HW: You mentioned control charts. Whose responsibility is it to develop these control charts?

WED: Is there a method by which you can ask for some education in that direction? Is that your question? Well, I think you ought to have a QC circle on that one, to ask that question.

Here's a man who wants to learn something about the control-chart method so he can improve his work and know what the heck he's doing. That's the gist of it.

The Deming statement concerning effectiveness of quality circles in the presence of quality control echoes sentiments of William Latzko of Irving Trust, who has written extensively on quality control in banking. In the December, 1981 issue of *Bank Administration* magazine, he points out that without quality control, quality circles have no way of assessing the importance of problems, or seeming problems, in work flow and productivity. As a result, they may treat as major issues what are merely occasional fluctuations in quality. Also, they have no way of measuring the impact of their own ideas for improvement.

Latzko also warns that some managers are wary of quality circles and regard them as a threat to their positions because, under such a system, ideas flow up from the bottom rather than down from on high. If these managers are first introduced to quality measurement and required to participate in it, as is the case at Irving Trust, they grasp the value of quality circles quickly.

In the preface of his book, "Guide to Quality Control," Kaoru Ishikawa described the initiation of QC circle activities in Japan. They were begun there to enable workers to study together the principles of statistical quality control. He pointed out that Japan's industrial workers are quantitatively among the world's finest, but that "further polishing is necessary for them to show their true brilliance and strength."

We don't ordinarily think of the U.S. hourly worker as being interested in quantitative procedures. Interestingly enough, however, they usually find it challenging when they're given the responsibility for charting the daily results of their own efforts. They have a sense of being in control and of not having always to take the blame when something goes wrong.

When Dr. Deming and I were visiting Johnston & Murphy, one of the first things they showed us were control charts hung up in constant view of everybody. The workers who met there with Dr. Deming were nearly all women. Among them was Inez Knott, Chief Quality Auditor, who told me following the meeting that she and others had been shown earlier a videotape of the NBC documentary "If Japan Can, Why Can't We?" featuring Dr. Deming. One can only speculate as to whether it was the showing of this tape that induced the immediate high level of receptivity in the audience. The fact that women tend to be more open than men may have contributed, as well as the fact that the J & M workers seem to feel relaxed with management, off the job at least. Generally, the audience warmed up quickly and almost immediately spoke of wanting to have pride in their work and to produce products of excellent quality. It was a theme I heard over and over.

These meetings of Dr. Deming with the hourly workers serve several purposes. First of all, their aim is to allow management to observe (firsthand or from a videotape made during the meeting) how the workers feel about working conditions and management policies and, also, what may be their most important problems.

A meeting of this type also provides a means for catharsis, by letting people talk about their gripes and discontentments. Perhaps most important, however, is that in arranging this confrontation with Dr. Deming, management is giving a sign that level of quality is important to them. If they follow through with further action, then the workers may come to feel that since the bosses care about delivering high quality products, there is a chance that such can be achieved. There's hope!

He then brought up the subject of slogans as a means of motivating the hourly personnel. The one he talked about in the exchange with the workers was, "Your work is your self portrait. Would you sign it?" On this occasion he mentioned, "Do it right the first time."

"It has a wonderful ring to it, but it helps nobody

whatever to do a better job."

The problem, of course, is that the slogan itself provides no methodology for attaining the excellent goal that it embodies. It provides no tools. Any increase in productivity wrought by such a slogan by itself can only be temporary. "In the end," Dr. Deming said, "the slogan advertises to the work force that management is helpless to solve the problems of the company. Do they need to advertise? The workers already know it."

Dr. Deming told me some of his thoughts about what companies could do to let their people know that they were concerned about quality and working to improve it.

> "They can put up posters every month, and explain what management is doing about the 14 points. They don't need to number the points or attach anyone's name to them. Just say what they're doing. For example, 'We're attempting to improve the quality of incoming materials. You may have seen the effect of it in your own work.' That would show that management is on the job. It would have a great effect, I think. It would show these workers that there is some use to try."

This sort of effect was achieved by a story in the June, 1981 issue of *Focus,* the monthly newsletter of Genesco, the parent corporation of Johnson and Murphy. The story concerns management's successful undertaking, under the direction of Dr. Deming, of incorporating "communicable" descriptions of responsibilities of workers at Genesco's Pulaski, Tennessee plant. It was necessary to do this before process control methods could be installed there.

After Dr. Deming had been brought in by James Harbour,

Genesco's president, department managers at Pulaski spent several months working with the people making shoes to determine what each operation required. These were not instructions in how to do the job, but rather a brief written statement of what results were required. When these operational descriptions were completed, they were posted in prominent places so that each operator could read what was expected from his or her operation.

Operators immediately became aware of just what they were supposed to be doing. Some found for the first time exactly how they contributed to the overall quality of the finished product.

Fentress Harney was one such employee. At the time the program was initiated, she had been with Genesco four years in what is called the lasting department. When her operational description was developed, Ms. Harney discovered that part of her function was to pull ½ inch of material around the bottom of the plastic mold around which a shoe is made. If this is not done, the shoe will most likely come apart after it has been worn a short while.

Properly, this type of defect cannot be found by inspecting the final product because it doesn't show. The defect is hidden. Therefore and because no one had ever explained to her the details of her responsibilities, Ms. Harney had never been aware of the ½-inch lasting allowance. Clearing up this problem obviously had an impact on customer satisfaction. And that it was reported in the Genesco newletter made rather an impression on the workers.

Ms. Harney's experience serves to call attention to the Deming Doctrine's point number 6, which involves training. When Dr. Deming says, as he often does, "The American worker doesn't know what his job is,'' he may be overstating the case. But the percentage of the U.S. workforce for which this is to some extent true would probably amaze the collective membership of the National Association of Manufacturers.

Dr. Ronald Ribler, an industrial psychologist and author of "Training Development Guide," told me of a specific instance in which a company resisted giving rudimentary training to critical personnel in favor of making a huge capital investment in a computer.

The case involved a plant of a very large U.S. company where integrated circuits were assembled, imbedded in plastic and then tested. In the testing, a large proportion of the i.c.'s were found to be faulty; and it turned out, after only cursory investigation, that the principal cause was that the people in the initial stage of the process had not been given sufficient explanation about polarity.

At the Yokogawa Hewlett Packard plant near Tokyo, we saw how a similar problem was overcome. There, the people who assembled integrated circuits were given some visual aids, together with like parts taped together with positive polarity on one side and negative, of course, on the other. This was one of the devices YHP has used to help the company achieve their amazingly low defect rate.

In the case Dr. Ribler told me about, management decided not to use this kind of approach. They opted, rather, to invest several hundred thousands of dollars in more sophisticated equipment for testing after the poor quality was irrevocably built in.

A policy that has an effect just as devastating as the resistance of management to giving training, is the incorporation of a "work standard." In one of our meetings, I asked Dr. Deming how this phenomenon, which he mentions in every interchange with hourly workers and which is the subject of one of the 14 points, came into being. His response began with a conjecture:

> "Well, I think there could have been somebody, probably some industrial engineer, who computed that the average person should be able to do so much per day, in 8 hours, so many per hour. And that became the standard. Management didn't have any more sense than to accept it, instead of helping the workers to improve productivity."

> "Now, the industrial engineer is absolutely vital to industry today, whether it be in service or in manufacturing. It is necessary to be able to have some kind of figure for your cost, and cost per unit for next year. Absolutely vital. But the trouble with the work standard is that there is nothing built into it to improve the process, nothing built into it to improve productivity. You are stuck with the original figure forever, and it is one of the surest ways to guarantee that American stuff will not be competitive."

The work standard is clearly a barrier to getting acquainted with the problems inherent in the process by means of control charts. It is a barrier to eliminating the problems and improving the process.

Dr. Deming told me about a talk he had had with an officer of a very large bank. They had hired a company to come in and set up work standards. A teller should be able to handle, on the average, so many customers per hour. A woman computing interest and penalties on loans should be able to do so many per hour. Card punching should be so many per hour for this kind of job, and so many per hour for another kind of job. And on through, for all the multitude of jobs that there are in a big bank, about which most people don't know anything.

There was not one word in these specifications about quality. "It wouldn't make any difference how many mistakes anybody made," he said, "not one word in there about how to improve. Improvement is therefore totally impossible. The existing process is preserved in concrete."

> "This is obviously wrong. People just don't think. Work standards are causing the country tremendous losses. They are on their way out, but it will take a long time to dislodge them."

I asked him how companies are managing to make the change.

> "They can't just pull out the rug. It will take a year or two to provide leadership, a supervisor who knows, by calculation of control limits, if possible, which if any of his people is in need of help."

A control chart can help the supervisor to find out why help is needed so that the problem can be addressed. If the system is in control, he or she can be a valuable aid to its improvement by taking a leadership role in finding out what makes it tick. Lack of leadership, together with maintenance of work standards, means the organization is stuck with the low levels of productivity defined by the standards.

> "It is clearly wrong to finish up an hour or two early.

People on the job know it. They know that the machine is there and the stuff is lying there ready for use. Somebody is paying interest on the inventory. They may not put it in this language, but they understand. They know very well that it is very poor management. They are not happy about it, but they do learn to use their time. The human race is an adapting race."

Oftentimes, the work standards that are imposed upon the hourly worker are consequences of the incorporation of a management style called "management-by-objective" or M.B.O., which is widely taught in business schools and is practiced by nearly every major U.S. corporation. Dr. Deming maintains that Western industry has been devastated by M.B.O., and its elimination is invoked in points 11b and 12b of the 1986 statement of the Deming philosophy.

The operating principles and implications of M.B.O. are discussed in some detail by Dr. Brian Joiner and Peter R. Scholtes in a report from the University of Wisconsin's Center for Quality and Productivity Improvement entitled "Total Quality Leadership Versus Management by Control." Joiner and Scholtes point out that management-by-objective is simple and consistent and is attributed by many for getting us where we are today. In this style of management, each manager, beginning at the top of an organization, is given certain numerical goals for the near term. Each of these managers, in turn, sets numerical goals and imposes controls on each of his or her subordinates. At the lower levels, these goals become quotas or work standards.

What Messrs. Joiner and Scholtes call the "underside" of M.B.O. arises from the fact that near-term countable accomplishments receive priority, even though an organization's survival may depend on long-term accomplishments, impossible to measure in the near term. Systems of controls and numerical goals without a long-term loftier purpose will tend to set up conflicts within an organization; one unit's short-term gains will be a result of controls that often will interfere and be in conflict with those of another unit.

"Engineers will rush products into production before they are ready. Purchasing will buy materials which the warehouse can't store and the people on the line can't use. Planners and policy-makers plan programs which service personnel aren't equipped to provide."

Dr. Deming tells us that to see the futility of M.B.O., one need only plot the variables on which the numerical goals are to be imposed. If any variable is in control and the goal pertaining to that variable lies beyond the present capability of the system, then it cannot be attained except through the possible destruction of other systems in the company.

"Recognition of the distinction between a stable system and an unstable one is vital for management. A stable system is one whose performance is predictable; it appears to be in statistical control.

"For example, if a plot of points shows the number of fires per month on the premises over two or three years has been stable, then only fundamental changes by the management will reduce the frequency of fires.

"It is instructive to look at a plot of proportion of people absent from the job week by week over the past two years. Does the plot show a stable system? If yes, then only the management can reduce it. Other helpful plots might be the number of complaints of customers, costs of warranty, sales, outgoing quality, scrap, rejections, accounts overdue by four weeks or more.''

Such plots make clear the futility and fallacy of management by the number, he says. What are needed in place of controls and numerical goals, Dr. Deming reminds us, are constant improvements, through the efforts of management, of design of the product and of the processes involved in the operation of the organization.

One of the many intrinsic elements of M.B.O. is the employee performance appraisal system, which rewards conformance to the built-in controls of management-by-objective, rather than nurturing and sustaining individual contributions to the continuous improvement of the operation of the organization.

In 1984, Donald E. Petersen, currently Ford's Chairman, explained why the Ford Motor Company was re-evaluating traditional views of performance appraisal:

> "We believe our personnel evaluation system is a possible barrier to continuous improvement and quality performance. We recognize that revisions are required, and an employee group is studying what actions should be taken.

> "We do know that the emphasis of any such system must be on developing teamwork throughout the corporation to meet customers' needs. There is untold waste of human resources with traditional evaluation systems.

> "The waste results from excessive internal competi-

tion, not getting to the root causes of problems, and reinventing the wheel — to name a couple of situations where teamwork should pay dividends.

"The point is that we have to be sure that our short-term operating procedures aren't roadblocks to reaching our long-term objectives. If you get the impression from what I've said that I think a substantial part of our competitive problem internally is in our systems and the way we operate the business, you've gotten an important part of my message."

Bill Scherkenbach, Ford's Director of Statistical Methods, maintains (see *Quality Progress,* April, 1985) that, like other aspects of management-by-objective, individual performance appraisal destroys teamwork and cooperation, fosters mediocrity, increases variability and focuses on the short term. In addition, it treats people like commodities and promotes fear and loss of self worth.

Teamwork is undermined because the traditional approach of management-by-objective demands that each employee of each department be evaluated on goals and objectives that apply to his or her department's function, say purchasing, finance or marketing, or perhaps engineering or manufacturing. When the goals of two different departments are in conflict, as they obviously very often will be, any cooperation between them exists in spite of the system, not because of it.

Hewlett-Packard C.E.O. John A. Young tells a story in which one of his company's quality managers observed an unexpected consequence of the evaluation of individuals on the basis of parochial goals. One day the manager was acting as a facilitator for two different groups of buyers who were identifying quality problems for study. Each group came up with a list of a hundred.

Because the quality manager's background was in production, he was amazed that neither group's list had identified late parts as a problem. From the perspective of the people in production, this was problem number one. When he asked one of the purchasing supervisors why neither of the two lists of problems had included late parts, the reply was, "Because we don't get measured or evaluated on them."

Mr. Young confides: "The overriding importance of performance measures and their effect on teamwork has caused some careful reappraisal at HP."

Even though competition, rather than teamwork, is implicitly encouraged by individual performance evaluation, mediocrity is fostered. Mr. Scherkenbach explains that because one either meets one's assigned objectives or does not, unambitious objectives are negotiated so that there is little risk of falling short. Attainments beyond the negotiated goals may be "banked" to use in the next period of evaluation.

This negotiation of mediocre goals is, incidentally, similar to that used for work standards, which as a result also promote suboptimal-level performance as the norm. When there is a demand for levels of output from hourly workers above the negotiated standard, overtime is required and costs are escalated. The existence of overtime pay adds a cost element to work standards that make them at least as onerous as individual performance appraisal.

In the evaluation of the performance of any individual, hourly worker by a supervisor or professional by a manager, a fundamental error nearly always made is that results are entirely under his or her control. In reality, the performance of anyone during any given interval of time will be for the most part determined by the random fluctuations of the many variables that govern the system in which the individual operates.

In other words, the process defining the system is very often in control, which means that individual performances are simply random outcomes. When this is the case, rewarding top performers can introduce more variability into the system by motivating those in the lower percentiles to emulate those singled out and rewarded. And even if those individuals who are below average do not try to change, they may be devastated by the stigma of being identified as being below average.

When performance has been exceptional, e.g. outside of control limits, or when one consistently, time after time, is above or below average, then some sort of recognition or special attention is due.

Joiner and Scholtes point out that when measurable controls or goals are unattainable or impractical, individuals and groups tend to fabricate conformance, which fosters guarded communications and more dishonesty. The greater the stress on reaching unattainable goals, especially when someone's career is on the line, the more likely it is that figures will be juggled.

"Management by control encourages an organization to look inward at its own structures rather than outward at the world in which the customer operates. Rather than delight in providing a product or service that works and satisfies the customer, the sense of accomplishment comes from meeting the controls. It becomes a self-reinforcing cycle. A manager or supervisor has a goal imposed on him or her. The manager works to meet that measure, however much distortion might occur at some other time or place in the organization. Meeting the short-term measurable goal is an indicator of the success of the individual and the success of the system of controls. Thus, there is fostered a Titanic-like complaisance about the invulnerability of the operation. When there finally is some awareness that the indicators of control may be focused on the wrong measurements, it's too late. The ship is going down and 'Nearer My God to Thee' is heard from the afterdeck.''

CHAPTER 5

BUYING QUALITY OUTPUT FROM SUPPLIERS

"It's a little like the tale of the roadside merchant who was asked to explain how he could sell rabbit sandwiches so cheap. 'Well,' he explained, 'I have to put in some horsemeat, too. But I mix them 50-50. One horse, one rabbit.'"

Darrell Huff in "How to Lie with Statistics"

During a visit to Washington in the spring of 1982, I heard Dr. Deming's thoughts about the price one pays when always buying from the lowest bidder. At the same time, he mentioned new requirements for statistical evidence of quality that some companies are finally beginning to impose upon their most important vendors.

He told me of one interesting example which dealt with the Washington Transit Authority. They, like other municipal transit authorities, could get federal money, which they badly needed, only if they would buy from the lowest bidder.

"They bought, a few years ago, several hundred new buses, and rattling around on Washington's streets, the glass in the side windows became almost opaque. You cannot see out. You can tell whether it's night or day, and you can observe that there is a street light in the vicinity, but you cannot see any scenery. It's all hidden.

"And who would make glass like that? Well, somebody did. And the seller can offer a good price on it; he's lucky if he can get anything for it."

Dr. Deming explained that this may have been part of an inventory that had already been rejected, and the seller could offer it at a much reduced price. "Now," he asked, "Who would buy it? Why the obvious victim would be someone like the Washington Municipal Transit Authority because they have no one there who can really gauge quality. Besides, they feel constrained to buy from the lowest bidder."

"To have somebody that knows something about quality, they'd have to pay money. Such people are high priced. But they would save untold sums of money. It requires only a third-grade drop-out to observe which price is the lowest, and he's the one who gets the job.

"There's a better way today. We're in a new economic age, which requires that suppliers give statistical evidence of quality in the form of control charts and evidence that they are working on all the 14 points. Purchasing managers now have a new job, and it will take them 5 years to learn it. I don't say everybody will take 5 years. Some will learn within a few months, some in a year. I know how long it takes people to learn. I've been a teacher for many years."

It's clear that Dr. Deming would like to see the ways of doing business change drastically because the old methods are outmoded. This will mean, in most cases, a dramatic reduction in the number of suppliers for any company. An American auto maker could easily have 4,000 vendors. One company estimated that they could reduce that number to 800. Dr. Deming says,

"This process will take about 5 years. I think that's about as fast as they can go."

"And then, in another 5 years, they can reduce the number to half of that. Now, that means that in most cases there will be only one vendor delivering any one particular part or material, because the problem is to find someone who can furnish evidence of quality. You must remember that I'm talking about critical and semi-critical materials and parts. The real problem lies with the purchase of anything that has to be made to order and that may have to be changed in 6 months, or less, anything that nobody knows how to make with certainty, anything the manufacture of which requires attention. The only way to buy them from here on is with evidence of quality. And that means physical evidence of quality, not by inspection, but by using the quality control charts of the suppliers.

"Supplier companies are using statistical methods for process control, with results that were not thought possible a few scant years ago. There are companies that make stampings and plastic parts to almost incredible tolerances without any defects.

"The way Americans have done business is usually by contract, the so-called purchase order, valid for a year. But nobody can really develop a good product on the basis of a contract for a year. Not with the investment that a company has to put into such development. It would be a very wasteful way of doing business.

"Now there is finally a strong movement to take my advice, namely, to have one vendor. In the first place, a company will usually be limited to one that can deliver evidence of quality in the form of control charts. It should be made a long-term deal. In Japan, it's forever. Without contract. They just don't change unless there's a very good reason, and then they would talk it over first to see what the problem is.''

Dr. Deming pointed out that a long-term contract permits the vendor to invest to the advantage of the customer company and improve the process continually — to make a better and better product at lower and lower cost. The supplier can then offer gradually decreasing costs over a period of years. Dr. Deming mentioned some of the other dividends of such an arrangement.

"One company I worked with decreased their inventory in process over a 13-month period by 15 million dollars, simply because of better quality of incoming parts and, hence, less rework all along the line.

"Now, not only does the customer get better quality, but the company's costs are so much lower. And that isn't all of it. There are hidden benefits that you don't see if you don't think. Space that this company was using for storing rework and scrap was now empty. They now may install new equipment — or expand existing equipment — or give people more room. They had been thinking of trying to rent a building not far away because they needed space. And now they have it free of charge, just as a bonus from better quality. No one thought of it in advance. And here it is, right in their laps. No wonder they're happy.''

The Ford Motor Company is one of the U.S. companies

trying hard to help their suppliers adopt and adhere to the Deming philosophy. In February, 1982, Ford held a 3-day Deming seminar for employees and 200 supplier executives. In introducing Dr. Deming, Don Petersen, Ford's president, spoke of the company's goals for enhancement of quality and improvement of productivity and then addressed the executives from the supplier firms. They would, to an ever growing extent in the future be considered "part of the Ford family," which was the way Mr. Petersen phrased it. Then he revealed Ford's goals for the supplier companies.

> "The need to accomplish in every other company the objectives that I have described is just as important as accomplishing them at Ford Motor Company. So I urge all of you from our suppliers to think along the same lines as we do at Ford. I want to assure you that we are in the process of making a major change when it comes to dealing with our supplying companies. My goal is that this will become truly a partnership effort, rather than the type of arm's-length relationship that has all too often been the way we have worked in the past. The fact that you are here is an excellent example of the need we all have to develop a stronger feeling of partnership to accomplish the overall goals of better quality and higher productivity. That is essential."

Less than 3 months after this conference at Ford, an article describing the initial results of Mr. Petersen's resolve and determination appeared in the *Los Angeles Times.* "Act Japanese, American Car Makers Tell Their Suppliers," the headline read.

Clinton D. Lauer, a Ford purchasing executive had submitted a report titled "Japanese Business Practices" to dozens of companies that sell components to Ford. The clear but unspoken message was that if their quality and productivity were not improved, they would lose Ford's business. As the *L.A. Times* put it:

"It was one small volley in the U.S. auto industry's war on a hidden but major part of its business — the network of more than 2,000 companies that make more than half the parts that go into cars.

"While much attention in the current slump has been focused on high labor cost, inefficient manufacturing techniques and free-market U.S. trade policies, the automotive giants have concluded that perhaps one-third of Japan's manufacturing superiority can be traced to inefficiencies in the enormous U.S. supplier industry."

Ford's Lauer told suppliers that unless they get competitive, they're going to find themselves out in the cold. Originally this meant only that they supply evidence of built-in quality in the form of control charts. Now Ford has begun to demand adherence to all 14 of Deming's points. As a result, the often rocky relationship between the car makers and their suppliers — from whom the car makers buy more than $40 billion worth of materials annually — is changing fundamentally. Critics, first among them Dr. Deming, say this change is long overdue. Now the suppliers are getting longer contracts and may be brought into the design stages for new cars, something they have always wanted. But they will have to slash prices and at the same time boost quality. Above all, the automakers want to hack away at what the *Los Angeles Times* calls the "$15-billion-plus albatross" — the day-to-day factory inventory of components awaiting installation in automobiles.

Chicago-based Quality Control consultant William Golomsky,

who has made over a hundred trips to the Orient to confer with Japanese industrialists, has pointed out that the zero-inventory system that is the pride of many Japanese firms is operable only if certain conditions are satisfied. Two of these conditions are that the manufacturing processes are in control and that the vendors are supplying extremely high quality products with little variability.

A more recent report from Ford concerning this issue was related by Ford's Petersen in a 1984 speech to the Society of Automotive Engineers. It involved a particular type of Ford transmission that was bought from two different suppliers. Although the auto company had verified that both were building to engineering specifications — at the asembly level and the component level — they found that customer reports indicated that one supplier's transmission performed significantly better than the other.

Measurement of the parts in both types of transmissions indicated that the one that performed better had less variability from piece to piece than did the other supplier's transmission. This demonstrated rather dramatically to Ford that reducing variability of incoming materials through statistical process control is one important element in making it possible to achieve continuous improvement in their processes.

Japanese auto makers, incidentally, have equity interest in practically all their supplier firms, each of which does business almost exclusively with its partner company. The Japanese system invites improved communications, close consultation on design, and a host of other efficient operational interactions, including a guarantee of controlled processes turning out critical parts with practically no defects. Ford and General Motors use many times more suppliers than Toyota and Nissan. Now, how-

139

ever, General Motors is beginning to absorb much of the Deming philosophy, first through his work with Pontiac and now through his consulting with the new Buick, Oldsmobile, Cadillac Division of G.M.

In 1982, the *L.A. Times* pointed to some foreseeable problems.

"But to implement Japanese-style relationships with scores of companies, critics say, Detroit and its support firms will have to smooth over an adversarial relationship that at times has matched, in depth of feeling at least, the pitched battles with the United Auto Workers union.

"The Big Three have routinely pitted suppliers against each other in bidding wars for contracts on identical parts, and suppliers complain of late-hour engineering changes ordered by Detroit that compromise the quality of components and create chaos in their plants."

Applied Magnetics in Goleta, California is initiating new quality-control policies for vendors in a way that is less dramatic than the approach of Detroit. I was told about this by Roy Reindl, their Director of Materials, during a George Washington University sponsored 4-day Deming seminar at Fisherman's Wharf in San Francisco in July 1982.

Reindl was the eighth person from Applied Magnetics to attend one of Dr. Deming's seminars. On the basis of what the others had learned, they were making a concerted effort to raise the quality of incoming parts.

They first identified vendors who supply parts that are critical or have a very high dollar volume in extremely complex components. Then they met with the chief executive officer, the chief financial officer, the head of production and the head of quality control for each of the vendors. The meetings were always at the vendor's facility and for the purpose of explaining the company's expectations of the supplier's responsibility to install statistical process control. Two or three months later, representatives from each company were invited to Goleta to be shown exactly where the product they made fit into the Applied Magnetics manufacturing process. The next step was a request that the suppliers, after an interval of time, report on their actions and progress.

When I asked Lloyd Nelson about Nashua's experiences in getting suppliers to control quality statistically, his reply was a pained one.

"This, I think, is the most difficult of all our activities. It is an impossible situation when you have a small vendor who can sell more than he can make. You buy 10 percent of his output, and you say, 'Let me tell you about quality control.' He says, 'Don't bother me. I'm too busy making money.'"

This way of thinking is clearly at the bottom of the problems of U.S. industry today. Lloyd Nelson, however, cited a couple of successful experiences. In one case Nashua sent an engineer to help a plastics company set up control charts on a particular item they were making, and the supplier ultimately hired the man to work for them.

"Now there was another company that was very aloof. They didn't want anything to do with quality control until quite recently when their defect rate went to 80 percent on a cover they were molding for us. Then they were ready to listen. They had no one to handle it, so we sent some people down to help them.

"They took data for 24 hours and then they plotted it. It was terrible! I said, 'Now listen, when you go back and talk to them, don't tell them how awful it is. You'll discourage them. Let's just focus on the really bad points. Look at what happened at the end of a shift. Tell them they have to find out what happened then.'

"You know, the second shift comes in and changes all the controls, because they want to run it their way. That happens a lot of the time.

"So they took it piece by piece. One of the fellows who was helping them said, 'Now, you see that. That shows something bad happened there.' And they answered, 'Yeah, that's probably such and such.' They cleaned that one up. Then there'd be another one, and they'd clean that one up. A little bit at a time. How do you eat an elephant? A bite at a time.''

CHAPTER 6

QUALITY AS A MANAGEMENT GOAL
THE KEY TO COMPETITIVE POSITION

"The basic cause of sickness in American industry is failure of top management to manage. Loss of market and resulting unemployment are not foreordained. They are not inevitable. They are not acceptable. The day is past when people in management need not know anything about management — by which I mean to include problems of procurement, production, supervision, training."

So said W. Edwards Deming in the preface of his book, "Quality, Productivity and Competitive Position." Dr. Deming has been telling us for many, many years that there is no career called "management" and that what has come to be known as "management theory" is leading us up the primrose path of quick payoffs. Such quick payoffs have become the primary goals of American business, partly because increased profits and dividends give those in charge an aura of success. But an emphasis on short-term profits can be insidiously destructive. It discourages company heads from risking innovation and from defining long-term goals for their organizations; and it results in a lack of sense of company identification and loyalty in both management and labor.

A manager with a bottom-line mentality will often increase the stockholders' return on investment by shortchanging resources like training, research and maintenance that can keep the firm in business far into the future. "Then," as Dr. Deming would say, "the manager moves on to destroy another company." Ironically, such an individual will most probably be offered large financial rewards to make the change in professional affiliation.

During a presentation in April, 1983 at Utah State University, Dr. Deming said, "Managers might as well live on an island and have financial figures sent to them. If that is what they use to run the company, they don't need to be at the plant." Or, as Ray Goldstein of Litton Data Systems interpreted Dr. Deming: "Top management needs to move off dead center and not indulge in running a business as if it were a spectator sport."

The theory which is designed to give the potential manager upward mobility is not one that can help anyone cultivate company loyalty and success over the long haul. The firm to be managed is thought of as a machine for turning out profits, rather than a means for long-term production of quality products and services that will let us live better materially and that will provide jobs for the future. Managers with fixations on short-term finance see their jobs as two-fold: first, somehow to get their employees to work harder and second, to decide where to allocate capital to attain the highest immediate returns. Thus, they stress better record keeping and more skillful union bargaining, and they use slogans and exhortations to stimulate an apathetic work force. When things go wrong, they blame tax policies, the bankers, the production workers and the unions, but never themselves.

The U.S. productivity crisis, long in the making but only recently becoming apparent, together with this country's persistently high rates of unemployment, have prompted researchers and pundits to look for policies on which to lay blame. Many agree with Dr. Deming that the fault lies, in large part, in the lack of a product-oriented approach to management and with the widespread application of the financially based management theory. For example, in an article appearing in *American Business* in February, 1982, Hyman Rickover, retired U.S. admiral, gave his views on this issue.

> "In searching for the causes of the apparent decline in U.S. productivity, we should not overlook the impact of the many professional administrators who, though trained in management, are unskilled in the technical aspects of their company. As a result, they manage largely in the terms they learned at school. Operational issues are quickly reduced to issues of numbers and dollars, to which management theory is applied."

Professor James Brian Quinn in "U.S. Leadership in Manufacturing," published by the National Academy of Engineering, joined in the complaint that manufacturing and technical managers have been replaced by would-be financial experts. They lacked "the intuitive feel for their process or product technologies" as well as "deep experience in technological innovation that bred comfort with major technological risks." Professor Quinn also said that control systems emphasizing near-term prospects "often undercut more basic technology building, quality improvement and human organizational development activities that would have given future strength. Most devastating was the effect on the not immediately measureable aspects of product quality. Few U.S. manufacturers chose to understand W.E. Deming's maxim that properly managed, high quality can actually cost less."

Substantial numbers of young men and women who were taught to master the practice of game theory and to perfect the technique of discounted cash flow have gone to the very top of many large corporations. There they have influenced a corporate culture that in 1982 experienced a lower rate of productivity growth than any of its major trading partners except Great Britain. Paul Solomon and Thomas Friedman suggested in their 1982 book "Trouble at the Top" that this approach is more likely to damage the efficiency of American business than to improve it. To produce a turnaround in American industry requires that corporate managers redirect their attention to turning out quality products, shouldering the risks of innovative activity and bringing personal and corporate goals into closer harmony.

Another consequence of so-called management theory is the elaborate system of management control consisting of the many layers of staff that have been built up in response to major structural changes in world markets and industries. At one time, half of the employees of the microprocessor manufacturer, Intel, were engaged in administration. When an engineer wanted a mechanical pencil, processing the order required twelve pieces of paper and 95 administrative steps. And this is a company that is only as old as Silicon Valley. One might note, too, that until very recently, Ford Motor Company had five more levels of management between the production worker and the company chairman than Toyota.

As the gap widens between the hourly workers and those in charge, a company becomes too diffuse and fragmented to generate team spirit and too unwieldly and bureaucratic to accommodate novel approaches to new problems. In such companies, professional managers concentrate on easily communicated month-to-month profit figures. Little attempt is made to report, through the many layers of staff, critical but less easily quantifiable information like product quality, worker morale and customer satisfaction. It is not surprising that American industry has been described as overmanaged and underled.

M.I.T.'s Dr. Myron Tribus pointed out that an important difference between Japan and the Western world lies in the way a corporation is regarded by its stockholders and its employees. In Japan, the physical assets of a company are not thought to belong exclusively to the stockholders, who are regarded as silent partners of the managers and workers. Profits are allocated, often equally, to the shareholders, to reinvestment and to management and workers. Japanese stocks seldom pay dividends of more than three percent since Japanese investors are interested in long-term capital growth more than in dividends.

If there is a downturn in Japanese business, the dividend is decreased, then decreased again. Then, management takes a cut in pay and finally, the hourly workers are given a cut. No one is turned out. A business downturn in most U.S. companies would usually precipitate actions in the reverse order: layoffs first and cuts in dividends last.

When there is an obsession at the top of a company with figures relating to short-term financial gains, the goal communicated to the production workers tends to be to produce as much as possible without consideration to quality of output. But there may be others in the company, quality assurance inspectors, for example, who have goals that conflict with production by the numbers. The result is dissension, disagreement and an increase in the normal discontent found in employees who work in a "production-goal" environment.

In any company where the emphasis is on simply turning out product — delays, rework, wasted human effort, wasted space and wasted material are the order of the day. Goals that invite the workers to cut corners will not lead to high quality competitive products. Management's behavior provides a pattern for others to follow.

For those competing with efficiently run firms, profits can come only through mortgaging the future by cutting costs of research and development, training, and consumer research. Often, though, management will be convinced that installation of some new, complex piece of equipment will be the solution to all their productivity problems. They believe the concept fostered by many economists that the way to increase productivity is to increase the level of capital investment per worker. "But," maintain Myron Tribus and J. Herbert Hollomon "if the productivity of capital is low because of poor management, greater capital investment will not increase productivity, . . . but may even decrease it."

The philosophy that bigger and more complex systems are necessarily more productive pervades the Department of Defense. There, more and more intricate weapon systems are ordered, with increasing demands for skilled labor. The result is usually increased unreliability. Mary Kaldor's 1982 book, "The Baroque Arsenal," shows how the U.S. leaders and industrialists have gotten themselves into the trap of escalating and ever more baffling complexity.

For a company following the Deming Doctrine, purchase of capital equipment is made only for well defined reasons; and the short-term bottom line is of secondary importance. In an organization that fully embraces the Deming philosophy, there is, for the C.E.O. and down through the ranks to the hourly personnel, a single goal that directs all activity. It is, quite simply, better and better products and/or services over time, resulting in satisfied customers. Implicit in this goal are efforts for continuing improvement in efficiency, with practically total elimination of waste and rework. Thus, a favorable bottom line will result from management's attention to the preceding lines.

It is important to get to the root of problems and to eliminate their causes. The philosophy is not one of crisis intervention, i.e., attempting to deal with symptoms when they become too severe. And allowing the workers to be part of the observing team and to participate in problem solving minimizes the costs of these activities. When problems have been identified and solved, then innovation can emerge. And when results of such innovation bring new problems, statistical techniques can be used to bring the system back under control at new, higher levels of productivity. It is a never ending process.

When Dr. Deming and I visited Ford's Dearborn headquarters in late 1982, we were escorted by Bill Scherkenbach, Ford's Director of Statistical Methods since early that year, and V.P. Jim Bakken. Bakken once said that Dr. Deming "is a burr under our saddle that keeps us riding tall." And it has resulted in an amazing improvement in Ford's market position. Ford led the U.S. auto industry's recovery.

Jim Bakken, at a seminar for statisticians held near Detroit in July 1985, told about evidence that led Ford to Dr. Deming. During his talk, Bakken showed a slide of what looked like three superimposed control charts pertaining to number of customer complaints per year for Ford, General Motors and Chrysler. The time span covered 1972 through 1980. The charts showed no apparent trends, but Chrysler's did seem to exhibit an inordinately large number of customer complaints in the late 1970s and did perhaps have some points out of control.

Next, he overlaid on that slide, one of the same sort — involving number of customer complaints for the years 1972 through 1980 for automobiles made by Japanese manufacturers. As in the other charts, years were indicated on the horizontal axis and number of complaints on the vertical axis; and what was clearly apparent for the Japanese cars was that the points were moving lower and lower year by year by year. There were fewer and fewer customer complaints as time progressed.

Jim Bakken said that when the management at Ford saw this, they realized that the competition from Japan came not because of that country's unique cultural heritage or the tradition of lifetime employment, their inclination for teamwork or any other of the explanations that analysts have used. Ford top management saw then in the early 1980s that what was putting the U.S. auto industry into a state of nearly terminal shock was the constant, never-ending improvement of the Japanese car manufacturers. Shortly after this revelation they looked up Dr. Deming and asked for his help.

The Deming-inspired "Ford Motor Company Operating Philosophy" is a very simple statement.

> "The operating philosophy of Ford Motor Company is to meet customer needs and expectations by establishing and maintaining an environment which encourages all employees to pursue never-ending improvement in the quality and productivity of products and services throughout the corporation, its supply base and its dealer organizations."

A note beneath the statement reads:

> "Management systems and styles, operating prece-

dents and technologies must be examined to determine whether they support or inhibit the concept of never-ending improvement in the quality and productivity of every aspect of our business. If not supportive, they must be modified or replaced by alternatives that are consistent with this philosophy.''

Transforming a company by inspiring managers, staff and workers to adhere to a philosophy of never ending improvement requires constant vigilance, hard work and visible affirmation and reaffirmation at the highest levels. The larger the organization and the more layers of staff there are between the head of the firm and the hourly workers, the longer it will take and the more difficult it will usually be.

A primary requirement is total commitment by top management to production of quality. Anything less dooms the process of transformation to failure. Thomas J. Peters and Robert H. Waterman, Jr., authors of the 1982 book, "In Search of Excellence," found that the most consistent quality among companies they rated as most successful is "obsession," a "seemingly unjustifiable overcommitment" to some form of quality, reliability and/or service. In opening remarks for a three-day Deming seminar for Ford employees and vendors, President Don Petersen conveyed his sense of commitment quite directly.

"As Chief Operating Officer of Ford Motor Company, I am committed to the use of statistical approaches to prevent quality defects. I am absolutely committed to that. All of you who are here from Ford Motor Company, I believe, by and large, report to me. Therefore, I would like to suggest that that should mean you would feel as committed as I do."

Ford's dramatic changes in attitude and outlook since exposure to the Deming Doctrine are reflected by later remarks by Mr. Petersen in the same talk:

> "It can be very difficult to make significant changes, especially when you have been in the habit of doing things differently for decades, and especially when the very success that brought you to positions you now hold was rooted in doing some things, frankly, the wrong way. It is going to be hard for you to accept that you were promoted for the wrong reasons a time or two."

The spirit of Petersen's remarks were echoed by Ford Chairman Philip Caldwell when I met him on the first morning of our visit to Ford's headquarters. Without the total commitment of Caldwell and Petersen, the introduction of the Deming philosophy into the Ford organization would have remained just that and never would have attained the success that it has. As *Time* magazine later quoted Caldwell:

> "There is no specific goal for improvement in our operations. We have a moving target. Once we reach a new level of quality, we set our sights on a higher level. This is the philosophy we received from Dr. W. Edwards Deming, the father of Japanese quality, and we embrace it fully."

This is the philosophy of "Never Ending Improvement," of which Dr. Deming speaks and which is the title of a film recently made by Ford about their new production principle.

In a presentation to the Society of Automotive Engineers in early 1983, Myron Tribus described an important consequence of acceptance by major corporations, like Ford, Nashua and

154

General Motors, of a philosophy of never ending improvement: Managers will not "parachute" into their positions from outside. They will be developed, over time, from within their companies through rotation around different parts of their organizations. Then, selection of top management can be made from among people who understand a company and know what it means to improve the quality of the output of the systems. This means harmonizing activities related to improving 1) the quality of the input — information, materials, delivery, storage; 2) the design and operation of the system, including the relation between the different departments; 3) the on-the-job training of all employees and 4) implementation of quality enhancement through statistical feedback.

One of the important policy changes made at Pontiac to put the Deming philosophy to work, i.e., the total switch in emphasis in their operations, involved particularly the shift in the role of the "Reliability" organization. It is no longer the responsibililty of Reliability personnel to inspect the product after defects are built in. They now respond and adjust to statistical signals and thus help in identifying what's wrong with the system and how it can be improved. Ford V.P. Jim Bakken calls this a shift "from defect detection to defect prevention."

There usually is a group with responsibilities similar to those of Pontiac's newly defined Reliability organization in any Japanese company that adopts "total" or "company-wide" quality control. This task force, normally called something like the "Total Quality Control Promotion Office," has as its aim to change the way workers and managers solve problems and the way they relate to the company and to each other.

At Pontiac, the Director of Reliability consolidates newly formed quality strategies, i.e., descriptions of what the various departments are doing over the short term and the long term towards implementation of the 14 points. Results expected and methods for measuring these results are also included in these quality strategies, which were developed with a great deal of employee involvement at all levels. The new approach provides guidance for day-to-day operations and helps everyone focus on the common goal of ever increasing quality.

Top management at Pontiac now promotes healthy interaction and teamwork among all departments. No longer is each organization considered to have its own "turf" and discouraged from interfering in the activities of other departments. The production system, made up of design, manufacturing, sales, service and administration, is treated as a whole, not as separate parts. For training in the new philosophy, Pontiac uses the "cascade" approach. Each management level is responsible for training at the next lower level.

Before Dr. Deming's arrival, reports *Fortune*, April 18, 1983, Pontiac had been struggling for years to improve quality, with disappointing results. General Manager Bill Hoglund says that Dr. Deming's initial work with Pontiac "shook the foundations of our approach to quality."

One of the several essential ingredients for never ending improvement in quality and productivity is that workers and management concerned with any particular stage of a manufacturing process or other system should get to know and learn from their customers, including those at the next stage. Managers working toward continuous improvement of quality know that customer feedback provides vital information that cannot be obtained from any other source. At one of the companies I visited with Dr. Deming, the president spoke of the firm he had recently left. There, he said, they were engaged in what

Dr. Deming calls "sub-optimization," every department doing its job efficiently while the company rushed headlong into bankruptcy. There was no communication between departments.

At Pontiac I talked with the people who design engines. For the first time, they were getting real feedback from the manufacturing people — what to avoid in their designs and what is desirable from the point of view of these individuals.

Results of consumer research and feedback from service departments can also, of course, signal needed improvements in both product and service. Many an innovative company gets its best ideas for both from customers, either directly or indirectly. And so they should. Without customers there is no need at all for turning out a product or providing a service. Dr. Deming points out, though, that it is not sufficient to study complaints. This, he says, is as bad as the supervisor who studies defectives to learn how to improve the process.

The companies Peters and Waterman call "excellent" in their book really stay close to their customers. "Other companies talk about it. They do it." And the "doing it" means that management has seen to it that results of studies about consumer preferences, marketability, etc., are distributed and used throughout the firm.

The studies are sometimes conducted in unorthodox and imaginative ways. For example, at Levi Strauss, top executives spend one Saturday a month selling blue jeans on the sales floor of a major customer. For these managers it is an eye opener to watch people decide to buy another manufacturer's jeans.

To obtain a similar kind of feedback, the chairman of

Campbell Soup sends executives to visit kitchens of housewives around the country to see how they prepare meals. He also insists that managers do their own grocery shopping to find out what happens in retail outfits.

At Ford, design engineers now meet regularly with several consumer panels to discuss vehicle and component function, as well as customer expectations. In his 1984 speech to the Society of Automotive Engineers, Ford's president (now chairman) Donald Petersen talked about one such session with a panel of women whose complaints about the usual inaccessability of spare tires led Ford to relocate the spare in both Ford's Tempo and Topaz models.

In this same speech, Mr. Petersen said that in Ford's new philosophy of never-ending improvement, one of the basic operating principles is customer focus, which means "redefining quality in the organization in customer terms, improving product feedback mechanisms, and developing innovative products and services that meet new customer needs."

"Essentially, everyone in the company is involved in a process that results in a product or service for a customer — whether that customer is a staff or operating function within the company or a car buyer or owner at a dealership.

"Therefore, all employees must think of their jobs in terms of meeting a customer's needs and expectations and strive for continuous improvement by identifying improvement opportunities and preventing problems."

Dr. Deming has given a warning that should be added to Mr. Petersen's words:

"It will not suffice to have customers that are merely satisfied. Satisfied customers switch, for no good reason, just to try something else. Why not? Profit and growth come from customers that boast about your product or service — the loyal customer. He requires no advertising or other persuasion, and he brings a friend along with him."

U.S. companies in the automobile industry appear to be more willing than others to accept the fact that past policies were self-destructive and that such courses of action must be abandoned. The recent real threat to Detroit's industrial base makes this attitude of U.S. car makers understandable. *U.S. News and World Report,* August 29, 1983, quoted David Cole, Director of Automotive Studies at the University of Michigan: "We're looking at a revolution, a new order in the industry. The alternative is the extinction of the business." He continued by saying that the automobile industry is in a transition period and that never before has change, a great deal of which revolves around quality, come about so rapidly.

Detroit's "bottoming out" is in some ways similar to Japan's postwar experience. As a matter of fact, many of the most successful Japanese firms of today have attained their outstanding success because of survival problems in the fairly recent past. For example, the Kajima Corporation, the Deming Prize winner that we visited in November 1982 had been forced to cope with the oil crisis at a time when a powerful leader of the company had just died. And the Rhythm Watch Company, another Prize winner, was forced to compete with quartz technology yielding accuracy previously only imagined.

Too many U.S. companies do not understand that they are experiencing a profound threat, but in the M.I.T. video tape of his "A Call to Arms" speech, William Conway cautions that unless businesses in this country embrace the Deming philosophy's 14 points, we will be left behind in the "third wave of the industrial revolution." Those who fail to heed the 14 points will be engulfed by the competitive wave created by those who do. Mr. Conway spoke to me of the "new way to manage a business," i.e., incorporation of the 14 points into the operating philosophy, as potentially yielding improvements in productivity of 50 to 200 percent.

Conway is credited with designing a technique he calls "imagineering." It consists of thinking of what a system would be if it were working perfectly and then comparing this concept of perfection with reality. The major points of difference show both problem areas and areas of opportunity for change.

Mr. Conway designed imagineering after much interaction with Dr. Deming. It is a most useful technique, especially for people who do not see that they have problems. Such people need to apply imagineering right down to the level of a flow chart and compare the real and imagined processes step by step, as they unfold, to see what and where the discrepancies are, in other words shifting from defect detection to defect prevention. This can be a small step toward the commitment to never ending progress that must be central to a company's goal if it is to become part of the current, the new industrial revolution.

Ford Motor Company Chairman Donald Petersen redeclared Ford's commitment to never ending progress in the pursuit of quality in an August 1986 letter published in *Autoweek*, Mr. Petersen first quoted a column by George Levy that had appeared in the July 28th issue of this same periodical:

"You don't hear so much about W. Edwards Deming

these days in Detroit. And you don't see so much effort—or progress—on the quality front from some American carmakers.''

In response to Mr Levy's remarks, Petersen wrote:

"I can't speak for our competitors, but let me assure you that Dr. Deming's influence continues to be strongly felt at Ford Motor Company and our commitment to improved quality is absolute.

"Ford's Mission, Values and Guiding Principles, published in the company's 1984 Annual Report, and our Ford Total Quality Excellence policy derive in large part from Dr. Deming's philosophy.

"... We meet with Dr. Deming at least once each month, and I personally discuss our progress on the quality front with him several times each year. Dr. Deming still conducts four-day quality seminars twice each year at Ford; more than 500 suppliers and employees have registered for his August 12-15 program.

"*Fortune* magazine, in an August 18 article 'Under the Spell of the Quality Gurus,' noted: 'By spreading Deming's philosophy throughout the company, Ford, in the view of consultants and market researchers who have made comparisons, has probably taken greater strides in improving quality than any other U.S. auto manufacturer. . . . A company that decides to take its quality consultant seriously can take off on a ride that will transform the whole corporate culture. As Ford found out, following the Deming path leads to a lot more than tinkering with the assembly line.'

161

"We are moving toward building a quality culture at Ford and the many changes that have been taking place here have their roots directly in Dr. Deming's teachings."

CHAPTER 7

THE MAKING OF THE MAN

"A man of genius makes no mistakes. His errors are volitional and are portals of discovery."

James Joyce in "Ulysses"

"There is no substitute for hard work."

Thomas Alva Edison

James Watt is rightfully credited with having set the industrial revolution in motion. Henry Ford, with his introduction of the assembly line, advanced it to the second phase. William Edwards Deming, who was born when Henry Ford was just getting his start, created the third phase, or "wave," as William Conway puts it, with a simple philosophy based on the age old concepts of measurement, communication and cooperation. This man, who was to have an enormous impact upon the development of industry in major countries of the West and the East, was born in Sioux City, Iowa on the 14th of October, 1900. He was named for his father William Albert and his mother, Pluma Irene Edwards Deming. Two and six years after the birth of Edwards, as he was called then, a brother and a sister came along.

The father traced his ancestry to one John Deming whose will was probated in Hartford, Connecticut in 1621 and whose family probably came from the Main River valley in Germany.

William Deming, before his marriage, had managed to obtain a somewhat informal education. During our recent conversations, Dr. Deming recalled his father's struggles and his own early years.

"To find anybody then with any education was most difficult. The teachers could be certified a year at a time. My father went to the school in Sioux City where a Mr. Atkinson taught and simply knocked on the door and asked if he could attend. How old he was I don't know, probably 15 or 16. He would do anything. He just had to go to school. Mr. Atkinson took him in and eventually provided what was then the equivalent of a high school education, beyond what's taught in high school today.

"In those days, you didn't go to law school. You read law. My father did this, but never became a lawyer. He never would tidy things up to pass the bar. He was well read, but he never, in fact, got a diploma in anything.

"When free land became available in Wyoming, he attempted to get some of it. And he succeeded. So we moved to Wyoming when I was six and a half.

"Those were hard days. We had land, but my father was no farmer. He did other kinds of work. We went to Cody, Wyoming first, and he worked with a law firm there. I think they still owe him money. And then, land opened up at Powell, which was by then only a grocery store and a railway station, tiny compared with Cody, and he got land there. It was supposedly free, though he paid the operation and maintenance on it. A lot of far-mers couldn't pay that. The government would have to take it back, or give them extensions, for forever, I think. They were very generous about that. It was a hard life,

166

but somehow we existed."

Their first house in Powell was a tar-paper shack, about the size of a freight car. Snow blew in through the crack in the door and in the windows, leaving an accumulation to be swept away in the morning. A red-hot coal-burning stove heated anything near it, but left water to freeze in a bucket not far away.

He remembers his mother taking him and his brother by the hands and praying for food. She took potato eyes, left over from planting in the spring, and cooked them.

Everybody in the Deming family worked. Edwards got a job when he was about 12 in a place that served meals. After school he would empty the boiler, get kindling for the next morning, bring in coal and do whatever else he was told to do. For that he got $1.25 a week, and he would save most of it.

His mother, having been educated in music in San Francisco, gave piano and voice lessons. Some of the students didn't have money to pay for the lessons, but they would bring along beef or something else the Deming family could use.

Powell had a population of about 200 at the time, and there were several hundred more people on farms around it. The first school that Edwards went to in Powell was ungraded, with pupils ranging from the first to the sixth grade. There was one teacher, and they all shared a single classroom.

The next year there were two teachers and a bigger building with two rooms. "But we learned," Dr. Deming said to me. "In fact we learned a whole lot better than they do now. You had to learn and work to get your schooling. They didn't gear it down to the average, and there were only 11 in my high school graduating class."

The fall semester after graduation, he entered the University of Wyoming. To get there, he took the train 500 miles to Cheyenne and 57 miles west to Laramie. He still remembers the mileages so well because some years after he left school, he became a consultant to the railways, helping to establish their rate structures.

There were no tuition fees then at Wyoming U., and he'd saved about 50 dollars for living expenses, which he supplemented by working. Periodically his father would send him a little bit of money, and occasionally his brother, too.

Dr. Deming told me about a chapter he'd written for a book entitled "Those Good Years at Wyoming U.", edited in 1965 by a fellow graduate. Later, he found a copy of his contribution:

"'Those Lean Years' is a better title than 'Those Good Years' for my campus experiences. It was in 1917 that I took the train from Powell to start off to Laramie. Laramie was a big place to me. I had been to Billings once or twice, so I was already accustomed to big-city life. I had seen Cheyenne only two hours between trains. I was brave enough to walk up and down a bit, keeping the Union Pacific station in view.

"Of course there were no taxis at the station in Laramie, or if there were, I certainly couldn't afford one. Powell had no taxis, not even electric lights. In fact, I had made $10 per month for years lighting the four or five gasoline street lights (five it was till a runaway team demolished one).

"Hand luggage and I arrived on foot at the University. On my first night I obtained a room at Appleby's, and stayed there two or three nights until I got located. I remember inquiring if the city water was fit to drink. I ended up in what was known as the Men's Commons: a large square frame house with no architectural imagination. The lower part was dining room and kitchen. The upstairs and possibly a third floor provided rooms for the boys, two, three, or four to a room, but only one to a bed, as I remember it. The food was good — at least I don't remember originating any complaints.

"First of all, I had to be on the lookout for a job. Subsistence would be the problem. I had some savings, but believed in conservation. I had thought it would be simple to make dollars and have some left over every week. Just to be sure, I arrived a day or two ahead of school to get in on the ground floor. Wages had been good in Powell, as a result of inflation from the War. I had been earning (collecting rather) $5 a day for irrigating. It turned out, though, that in Laramie things were different. I learned the hard way something important — competition. The best that the boys could do was 25¢ an hour if they could find work at all.

"I called on the President of the University, Dr. Alven Nelson, a man with a kind heart, as all know who remember him. He suggested that I consult the head janitor, Mr. John Prahl. John put me to work almost immediately. He gave me five different jobs during the week, with odd items part of Saturday. One morning I was to sweep the rural school. Another morning I was to wipe the tile floor in the main hall, and the other three gave me acquaintance with more buildings.

169

"On my first experience with the tile floor in the main hall, what I did was to scatter soapy water from a bucket all over the floor. I was very thorough; every square inch got soaped. No one had told me to wipe it up. I thought that it would dry up. When the students began to arrive, somewhere around eight, the floor was a hazard. The report came back to me from a dozen sources during the day that John Prahl was looking for me.

"Another job was behind the soda fountain at a drug store. Somehow or other, I muddled through, though customers must have been amazed at the new concoctions. Some boys obtained work on the Union Pacific Railway on night shifts at various jobs. Two or three boys would take a job together. The railway was very accommodating in that respect. It was a hard deal, being on the job eight hours at a stretch, even if only every other night. I preferred shorter hours and shorter pay.

"The refinery, when it came to town much later (1919 or 1920) when I was about to graduate, provided work for a number of people. One summer I stayed in Laramie and worked for Mr. A. Hitchcock repainting and staining the new Commons on the inside, and working at the refinery cleaning out the boilers. The work was not very heavy, but I remember being very tired at the end of the 16th hour after two consecutive shifts.

"There were many diversions such as singing in the choir at the Cathedral under the direction of Mr. Roger Frisbie, who was indeed a fine organist and choir master. I was on the job there Sunday morning and again at night, and at rehearsal once a week. Then there was the band under Professor Bellis. It was slyly whispered that if one did good work in the band, he would be sure to pass his courses in physics. Unfortunately, I took the basic course in physics before I joined the band, so I had to earn the grade. I had had musical education, but elected to play drums and tympani in the band. The band took a trip on the Union Pacific to Hanna, Rawlins, Rock Springs and Green River, and by the time I had hauled all those drums and tympani from the train to the concert hall and back again in all those towns, I decided that it would be better to play a smaller instrument, whereupon next year I played the piccolo.''

Music has always been an integral part of Dr. Deming's life. His favorite instruments today are the piano and the organ, both of which his mother taught him to play. And he sang in church choirs until travel made rehearsal impossible.

When he finally settled in Washington, he began to study voice and theory with Dr. James Dickinson. Later, Russell Woollen became his musical mentor. When he started to compose, it was religious music. Two of his masses are performed in churches in Washington. Because of his many lecturing and consulting commitments today, work on his music must be done late at night when other duties are not pressing. This is in keeping with the habits of his early days. The essay on the "good lean years" shows us that even then his life centered around working, contributing and learning.

After Edwards graduated from Wyoming University in 1921, he stayed there another year to study mathematics and help teach engineering and the preparation of engines for test.

"One day I got a letter out of the blue asking me to come to the Colorado School of Mines and teach physics, my main qualification being that I was somewhat talented on the flute. The way the letter read, I remember, was that I was known to be a good flute player, and the Professor of Physics would like to have a band.

"I wasn't that good at the flute, but I did want to get that job; so I practiced hard and made the grade. I was at the Colorado School of Mines for two years, teaching physics."

After he'd finished teaching the first year at the Colorado School of Mines, he took a summer job with the Denver Engineering Works to do drafting. Although he was a pretty good draftsman, he thought there must be better ways to earn a living than by pushing a pencil.

He decided to get a Master's degree in mathematics and physics at the University of Colorado at Boulder. He would take courses there in the summers and correspondence courses during the school year. He was a hard working student and still has his notes on "Heaviside's Operational Methods," for the analysis of electromagnetic communication theory. In one instance there was an implication that he may have improved on Heaviside's Methods. Notes from his instructor said, "Your answers are correct; your methods are right — astounding, to put it mildly!"

At the University Edwards met Agnes Belle, a pretty school teacher whose parents had come from Scotland. After a year's courtship they were married.

About the end of 1924, Oliver C. Lester, Professor of Physics at the University of Colorado, suggested that Edwards ought to go to Yale. Dr. Lester had studied there under Willard

Gibbs and other famous mathematicians and physicists. Deming had never thought of such a thing. "I thought Professor Lester had lost his mind," he told me. But Dr. Lester wrote to Yale on his behalf, and in response there was a letter, which Dr. Deming still has, offering free tuition and a job as a part-time instructor at $1000 per year.

Many people brought a lot of new ideas to Yale at that time, most of them controversial because they represented modern physics. There was Arthur Ruark and there was W.F.G. Swann. It was a good time to be at Yale.

Many times he expressed his feelings about the value of spending time listening to great scholars. "One can be inspired by their greatness and see the creative process at work," he told me.

While he was at Yale, he worked summers at the very large Western Electric Hawthorne plant in Chicago, doing research on telephone transmitters.

"Working there was a great experience, but it was a terrible place. The first thing my supervisor, Mr. Chester M. Coulter, told me when I arrived on the scene was not to get caught on the stairway when the whistle blew. 'You'd get trampled to death with those women coming down the steps, like a dam or a reservoir broken loose.' I enjoyed my work, but made no contribution to Western Electric, I'm sure. I got $18.50 a week the first year and saved $6 or $7 of it.

"Research was fascinating to me, and I worked with wonderful people. One was a Dr. Hal Fruth, whose desk was close to mine. There were no offices, merely desks.

173

The two of us spent a lot of time together, at noon, after hours, evenings, and he told me some things that have affected my way of thinking profoundly in certain areas. The work that I do with companies today uses some of his precepts. One of the most significant ones he taught me was imbedded in a conversation in which he told me, 'When you get your degree from Yale, this company will offer you a job, maybe at $9000.' I thought this man was gone! Why, I'd never heard of such a thing! Remember, these were gold dollars. 'But,' he said to me, 'not because they think they will need anybody at $9000. There are plenty of men worth $9000. But you might develop into somebody they would pay $50,000 — or even $60,000. Such men are scarce. And if they offer you a job, it's because they think you might develop.'

"Now that is the way a statistical organization ought to be run, in any company, and I insist upon it. There must be statistical leadership, such as Morris Hansen provided it at the Bureau of the Census. He was a leader of unquestioned ability. He didn't need people who were merely good; he needed people who would grow in knowledge and get better and better.

"The scarcest thing in anybody's company is knowledge. A company that doesn't nurture knowledge is not worth working for. People should get better. You cannot just remain good. You cannot remain just a good statistician. You cannot just remain a good chemist. You either deteriorate, disintegrate, and become part of the crowd, or you get better. And a company has an obligation to see that people get better. Very few companies are doing that, very few. In statistics they do it where I consult.

174

"At Western Electric there was a Dr. H. Rossbacher, who taught me another important lesson. His job was three levels above the rest of us, but we talked as we rode the train together now and then. He was a very kind man, 'though a bit aloof.

"He would get angry when someone would explain to him that 'Mr. So and So's work is very interesting, but it's too theoretical. He's not a practical man.' Dr. Rossbacher would hit the ceiling. He said, 'You just don't know that it has no use when you don't understand it? If you understood it, you might find it useful.'

"One never knows what's practical. If you understand it, you can use it — sometime. I have never learned anything that I haven't eventually used. It's just a matter of understanding it well enough. Dr. Rossbacher was so right! Where do you find men like him today? There are very few. Today everyone wants someone practical."

Sometimes Dr. Deming tried to inject some humor into our conversations, even when he talked about statisticians. "There are only two kinds of statisticians," he says, "just as there are five kinds of horses."

"You didn't know about the five kinds of horses? Well, there are saw horses, clothes horses, hobby horses, Charlie horses and nightmares. But there are only two kinds of statisticians. First, there's the mathematical statistician, whose interest has to do strictly with theory. If you get to talk with that person about a problem, it may astound you to discover how much he or she can contribute. But this individual doesn't want to get involved with the practical problem. Now that's the really important person because his or her work defines the boundaries of knowledge. Experience teaches nothing without theory.

"And then there are the theoretical statisticians. They try to guide their work with theory; at times they may even contribute to theory. But they know when they need help. That's what I'm attempting to be, trying to guide my work with theory.

"I'm known as a practical man, but don't claim to be one. The practical man was defined by the great Thomas Henry Huxley as the man who practices the errors of his forefathers. I don't want to do that."

I asked him how he came to be a statistician, after his years of training in mathematics and physics. His answer was quite involved.

"Well now, that's a very difficult question. I don't know if I have a good answer. But I don't know who else could answer it. Courses in engineering and surveying led me to the theory of errors, and in studying physics and mathematics, I learned a lot of probability. Kinetic theory of gases is a theory of probability. So are thermodynamics and astronomy. And so is geodesy, involving measurement of the earth's surface for the purpose of figuring the curvature or other characteristics of the earth. It makes use of 'least squares'. And I had very good teachers in least squares. That was, by the way, one of the courses I had by correspondence when I was in Colorado.

"When I saw some of these things in statistical papers, I recognized them. But in my then juvenile mind, I couldn't believe that anyone could be so naive as not to know the history of the subject. If I just open my old geodesy text at random, you will see things that are familiar, for instance, a result concerning the distribution of the sample variance rediscovered by Gossett in 1908. This text, written in German by Czuber in 1891, was used on the European continent before 1900.

"Sir Ronald Fisher also independently derived a lot of what was already in the book on geodesy, and in books by Czuber and by Helmert, who was head of the observatory at Aachen.

"I studied all of these books. When problems came up, I just found myself able to work on them. To help people. This happened at the Department of Agriculture where I went to work after I finished the requirements for my Ph.D. in 1928.

"I finished up my academic courses and then during the last few weeks of the academic year I started to work on a problem that Professor Page, my advisor, thought would make an excellent thesis topic. It was very interesting, and I did the whole thing in five weeks and typed it besides. It explained, after a fashion, at any rate, the packing effect of the helium atom, which weighs more than the 4 hydrogen atoms that comprise it.

"When people had problems with experimental data, I just worked on them and found myself able to make a contribution, of thought anyway. I don't know if I improved the results any. I just found myself doing these things, knowing a little bit about it from the books that I had studied, even though a lot of it had not yet been published in the statistical literature. And I suppose that's the way I got eased into it."

Dr. Deming began his career in government as a mathematical physicist in the Fixed Nitrogen Research Laboratory of the U.S. Department of Agriculture (USDA) in 1928, and he remained in that position until 1939. His 38 publications during that period had to do principally with the physical properties of matter. For example, there was a series of 6 papers on "Some Physical Properties of Compressed Gases" published in the *Physical Review.* But there were several that reflected his interest in statistical methodology and marked the beginning of his influence in this area of investigation.

Analysis of results of experimental work in bacteriology and chemistry gave him a chance to learn more about the statistical adjustment of data. There were 3 papers on "The Application of Least Squares," published in the *Philosophical Magazine.* And in his book, "Statistical Adjustment of Data," published in 1943, he brought together, in readily usable form, the substance of these papers and of the earlier literature and his own studies on the subject. This text is still frequently consulted for guidance on the application of the method of least squares in various different situations.

It was during this time, in 1930, and shortly after the Demings had adopted a daughter, Dorothy, that Agnes Deming died. The loss made him work even harder.

Dr. Deming was a special lecturer on mathematics and statistics in the Graduate School of the National Bureau of Standards from 1930 through 1946. His courses, given from 8 to 9 A.M. at the Bureau, later inspired many lectures and articles by his students. And these paved the way for the establishment in 1947 of the Statistical Engineering Laboratory within the Bureau of Standards.

Some time in 1927 there was a requirement for a researcher to help Dr. Deming at the Fixed Nitrogen Research Laboratory at the USDA. From among several applicants, a young woman named Lola Shupe was selected, and she and Dr. Deming wrote several papers together. In 1931 Lola obtained her master's degree in mathematics, and in 1932 she and Dr. Deming were married. Lola was a mother to Dorothy and later had two daughters of her own, Diana and Linda. She retired from government service in 1967.

From 1933 through 1953, Dr. Deming was Head of the Department of Mathematics and Statistics of the Graduate School of the USDA and made major contributions to the mathematical and statistical education of a whole generation.

"I would get people to give courses. For example, I got Shohat, the Russian mathematician at the University of Pennsylvania, to come and give a course in infinite processes. He came down from Philadelphia once a week the whole semester. And I got other people to teach, Bill Madow, Morris Hansen and Bill Hurwitz from the Bureau of the Census, among others. And then I gave courses on statistical inference and least squares.

"We would send out postal cards and make calls whenever anybody came to town. We would even talk to one another. Somebody developed something, and we'd have a seminar. But always, when anybody famous came to town, we would get him to lecture. Fisher came twice, and Wishart came several times from Cambridge."

179

In 1936, Dr. Deming went to London to study the theory of statistics with Ronald Aylmer Fisher at University College, the University of London. He told me a little of that experience.

"From Fisher you learned how to think, how a great mind works. He'd come in with a new result, the ink not yet dry, and try to explain what he was doing. It was dark and cold, and I could hardly see the blackboard, and I couldn't understand what he said.

"He would make mistakes. And then he would call someone who was in the front row, to help him through these mistakes."

As a result of having been at University College, Dr. Deming was able to arrange for Dr. Jerzy Neyman, who was a visiting lecturer there, to be the principal speaker at conferences on mathematical statistics at the USDA Graduate School in April 1937.

Neyman had been Head of the Biometrics Laboratory of the Necki Institute in Warsaw, Poland. While at University College, he read, at a meeting of the Royal Statistical Society, a revolutionary paper, "On the Two Different Aspects of the Representative Method: the Method of Stratified Sampling and the Method of Purposive Selection." This paper marked the beginning of a new era in sampling from a finite population in which every stratum is sampled. Dr. Deming attended some of Neyman's lectures in London, and arranged for Neyman's visit to the United States in 1937.

Sampling studies and sample surveys had been used by some agencies of the U.S. Government in the 1920's, notably by the Department of Agriculture, the Bureau of Labor Statistics and the Internal Revenue Service; but there had been very few examples based on true probability, i.e., stratified, sampling methods before 1933, when the New Deal undertook a massive program to speed reform and recovery. The Committee on Government Statistics and Information Services was established to provide new statistical data series and improve existing ones so that the new programs could be operated effectively and efficiently.

Dr. Deming took pains to ensure that Neyman's April, 1937 lectures were well attended by U.S. Government statisticians. Consequently, they made a tremendous impact, especially the conference "On Statistical Methods in Social and Economic Research: Census by Sampling and Other Problems," in which Neyman called attention in a forceful way to the basic and novel features of his 1934 article.

Dr. Deming worked an entire year to produce the book, "Lectures and Conferences on Mathematical Statistics." In the years to come, it had a tremendous impact on sampling theory.

The participants in the conference quickly recognized that Neyman's approach opened the door to accurate sampling error calculations and to near optimal sample designs for a host of U.S. Government statistical programs. The WPA thus gave it a trial later that year in the November, 1937 Check Census of Unemployment. The use of his method of confidence intervals and detailed presentations of error calculations in the ensuing publications marked a major step forward in U.S. Government statistical practice.

By the time the volume giving the results of the survey was published, the staff of the Bureau of the Census was already working on plans for the 1940 Population Census. Users of census data have always wanted more information than can possibly be provided with a normal budget, and in 1940 the demands were larger than ever before. Many of the users of census data were willing to accept sample results, but some of the old timers at the Bureau were opposed to the idea of sampling. "Sampling was abhorred," Dr. Deming told me, "because the Census had always been complete. It couldn't be anything other than complete. But sampling was in the air."

The final decision rested with Secretary of Commerce Harry Hopkins. After listening to the arguments pro and con, Hopkins decided in favor of sampling. This meant, of course, that the Bureau would need some expert help in designing the sampling procedure that would be used in the 1940 population census. "Well," Dr. Deming told me, "one day in 1939 the telephone rang, and it was Dr. Philip Hauser, the Assistant Director of the Census Bureau, wanting to talk with me about a job. And I said, 'Right Away!'"

And so he joined the Bureau of the Census as Head Mathematician and Advisor in Sampling. As in the case of the 1937 Check Census of Unemployment, the sample was tabulated before the full count tabulations were made. The advantages of the sampling procedure turned out to be even greater than expected. A report on methods, the back-up research and the advantages gained through the use of the sampling procedure was published in the December, 1940 issue of the *Journal of the American Statistical Association*. Sampling in the U.S. Government programs was here to stay.

After leaving the Bureau of the Census in 1946, Dr. Deming opened his office in Washington, D.C. as a Consultant in Statistical Studies. And he embarked upon the crusade which led to the renaissance of industry in Japan, to world prominence and finally to recognition in his own country, including five honorary doctorates. At the same time that he set up his consulting office in Washington, he joined the Graduate School of Business Administration at New York University as a full professor. Before he "retired" from NYU in 1975 to become Professor Emeritus, he regularly taught two courses in survey sampling and one in quality control; and, too, he served as advisor to about a hundred students who earned their master's and doctoral degrees. I asked him on one occasion if NYU didn't have some sort of policy concerning retirement of academic and other personnel at age 65 or 70. His response was, "Well, if they did have, they didn't tell me about it."

The fact is that he is still teaching at NYU and is still directing studies of graduate students. But this makes up only a small fraction of his activities. At an age when he might be expected to spend a great deal of time resting on his well earned laurels and reflecting on the new economic age that has resulted from his insight and vision, Dr. Deming is on the road from his long-time home in Washington, D.C. with a back-breaking schedule that only a few stalwart individuals could withstand. Between frequent visits to his major clients and not so frequent visits to the others, he finds time to give within a year, singlehandedly, about 23 four-day seminars on "Methods for Management of Productivity and Quality" or "Quality, Productivity and Competitive Position." He has also completed his latest book, used as a text for these seminars. Dr. Deming is imbued with a missionary zeal in imparting the message in which he and a host of disciples so strongly believe.